LIMITED EDITION

CATCH FIRE

How to Ignite Your Own Economy

DOUGLAS SCOTT NELSON

NEW YORK

Catch Fire
How to Ignite Your Own Economy

by Doug Nelson
© 2010, 2011 Doug Nelson. All rights reserved.

ISBN 978-1-60037-528-6 Paperback
ISBN 978-1-61448-007-5 ePub Version
Library of Congress Control Number: 2011927220

Published by:
MORGAN JAMES PUBLISHING
The Entrepreneurial Publisher
5 Penn Plaza, 23rd Floor
New York City, New York 10001
(212) 655-5470 Office
(516) 908-4496 Fax
www.MorganJamesPublishing.com

Editor: Tyler R. Tichelaar, Ph.D.

Cover Design/Interior Layout:
Fusion Creative Works,
www.fusioncw.com

Dedication

I dedicate this book to all those who are
committed to their dreams.

Acknowledgements

I want to take a moment to thank some very important people.

My wife, Melanie, who is literally the brains, the beauty and the boss behind all of this. This is as much her book and accomplishment as it is mine.

My son, Avery, for continuing to be one of my greatest teachers.

Tim Polk, for being a big part in helping to make this book what it is today!

Mark Rothstein, Stewart Welch III, and Dino Watt for contributing your gifts to this book and my life. I truly appreciate you and our common understanding of the concepts of win-win and brotherhood.

A special thanks to T. Harv Eker for his support and believing in me when there wasn't a reason to.

And finally, thank you to all those who have been cheering me on during this process and to my critics who have helped in making me who I am today.

Thank you.

Contents

Acknowledgements   v

Foreword: Garrett Gunderson   ix

Introduction   1

PART 1: How I Caught Fire   **5**

Chapter 1: How I Caught Fire   7

Chapter 2: Ka-BOOM   9

Chapter 3: Poor Me   15

Chapter 4: THE vs. MY Economy   21

PART 2: The Problem   **31**

Chapter 5: Myth Busting   33

Chapter 6: The Three Hands in Your Pocket   43

PART 3: The Solution   **67**

Chapter 7: The Scoreboard and Playbook   69

Chapter 8: Mind Your Own Business   89

Chapter 9: Be a Tool   103

PART 4: Size Matters   **127**

Contributors

   Mark Rothstein: Increase Your Tax IQ   131

   Stewart Welch, III: Asset Protection   145

   Dino Watt: Relationships   159

   Melanie Nelson: A Healthy You   173

Epilogue   203

About this Book   205

About Doug Nelson   207

Foreword

I am sooo reluctant to ever do an endorsement (especially a foreword) as it is rare to have people think clearly and have a full premise without contradictions or holes in their philosophy or teachings. It is also essential for me to read anything I support. Well, I am a bit embarrassed that I have kept this book from you due to the delays on my part because I procrastinated, that is until I was inspired by Doug's story. See, there are people out there that dream of an easy life, if they could only have financial freedom... on the other hand there are those that realize that freedom allows them to give more and have a greater positive impact in the world. This is what happens when money is put in its proper place, behind purpose. What I mean by the previous statement is money becomes an asset rather than a liability. It is only when money isn't the primary reason or excuse for people doing or not doing something that real power and freedom can come about. This is who Doug is, what he represents and what he will teach you in this book, which is why I am honored to write this foreword.

If you wake up worried about money or in a financial prison, Chapter 7 will be of huge significance for you. It may be hard to hear, but easier to do something about it and deal with the reality. I love that Doug has nailed it when it comes to what really has to happen to get out of (and stay out of) debt. He talks about the root of debt and unless you know this, debt will always be in your life. You will learn not to borrow to consume, to eliminate all things that move you backwards, and only borrow to invest when you have certainty (otherwise it is gambling). Although I have different strategies around debt and debt management, Doug and I agree that most miss the root of what causes debt and that is why it is never resolved. There are plenty of books merely about sacrificing, saving and deferring your life to the future, but Doug is wise in knowing that it isn't merely about defense, it is about offense as well.

Doug gives great counsel of living within your means and the great news about you investing in this book is it gives you an opportunity to catch fire and increase your means. You will learn that it is about the investor not just the investment.

Doug has nailed it when it comes to what you can do about the economy. He will not only illustrate the concept that destroys wealth, but he dismantles it. If you are chasing net worth, this will revolutionize your life.

Also, before you put another dollar in a bank or an investment, you have to read about the issues surrounding our banks and banking system. Doug articulates the major problem of protecting our money with our money, and the concept of imaginary money.

Every single American has to see what is shown when it comes to the amount of tax we pay. See, this book won't skirt the issue to make people feel warm and fuzzy. You will learn some things that are very difficult to see, how banking actually works, what inflation is and the possible ramifications....... the good news is you learn about the most important economy for YOU.

So how did we get in this mess? Why are there so many numb people? Why don't more people get it? The secret is in the following pages. This book isn't just pointing out the problems either (although it shows you behind the curtain); it has a major focus on what to do. It gives you questions to ask of yourself and gives you ways to apply this to your life and discover what you can do. Hell, the Essential Skills section is worth the investment in this book alone.

Oh yeah, huge bonus for anyone in a relationship, Dino Watt gives you the essentials to give you the real riches in life.

So what I can tell you is that everyone has a Soul Purpose, but not everyone is living it. You have one, will you live yours? Read this book and the odds are now in your favor.

Garrett B. Gunderson,
New York Times Bestselling Author of
Killing Sacred Cows

Introduction

My name is Doug Nelson, a.k.a. the Burnt Guy. We'll get to the story of why I'm called the Burnt Guy shortly. For now, I think it's important that you know this about me: when it comes to commonly held beliefs and education regarding investing, retirement accounts, the stock market and so on, I'm what you might call a *contrarian*—I strongly believe that the vast amount of information we have been told about retirement, financial fitness, investing and so on is *bullshit!* That's right, bullshit.

Almost all our entire financial and retirement systems have been rigged. By whom? By the individuals and institutions that have created them. These systems are designed to siphon your hard-earned money so they can play their games with it—charge their fees, their commissions, and their charge-backs, and ultimately *make huge profits whether you make any money or not.* They don't really care about your gains; all they care about is getting their hands on your money. Your money is simply the raw material getting fed into this giant economic furnace, where they get the heat… and you're lucky if there are some coals left over to keep you warm. Then adding insult to injury, when they screw up on a colossal level and lose trillions of dollars of your money, "we" bail them out… yet they still get paid their huge bonuses.

Our system is full of fallacies and faults, creating a vicious cycle where the vast majority of us continue to work harder and harder yet fall further and further behind. The bottom line is this: the myth of working hard, saving for retirement, and then living a life of leisure—golfing in Florida, bouncing grandchildren on your knee, or buying one of those land yachts and clogging up a freeway exit—is truly, for most Americans, A BIG FAT LIE! The brochure is NOT as promised, folks!

According to most statistics:

95 percent of Americans retire without financial freedom.

What's more, more than half of retired Americans live on less than $10,000 a year plus Social Security benefits.

Stinks, doesn't it?

Here's the good news: You CAN achieve financial freedom. I've done it. I'm about to share with you how you can become financially free. Now, it's going to take some effort on your part, some new thinking and new beliefs and above all some new actions. It won't be easy—nothing of significance is. But you can do it, that I promise you.

Let's get one thing straight right now before we move on—this isn't about becoming a "gazillionaire." It's not about showing off to your neighbors, nor flaunting your wealth through flashy cars or expensive jewelry (although I have nothing against either of those two things!). This is about putting yourself in a position where you are financially bulletproof, that no matter what happens in your industry, our economy, or in life, you won't have to base your decisions on money. Financially free people get EDUCATED (and not the standard way). They understand how money works. They know the rules of the game and play to win, and because of these things they get to spend significant time with their families and loved ones. Financially free people don't take a day off, we don't take a week or two off—we take whole *seasons* off. Visualize that for a moment… taking, say, the summer off to travel, play, whatever…all the time knowing that you still have money flowing into your bank accounts. And let me add that there is something spiritual about getting up every morning and knowing that whatever I do today is because I made the *choice* to do it. Pretty cool, isn't it? If this appeals to you, then this is definitely the book for you.

You can escape the financial prison and set yourself free. Keep reading, and I will show you how.

To your Health, Wealth and Freedom

Doug Nelson

PART 1

How I Caught Fire

CHAPTER 1

How I Caught Fire

Ever have one of "those" days? You know, the kind of day when nothing seems to go right. Have you had one lately? Perhaps you're even thinking that *today* could be one of those days.

Like most people, I've had a few of "those" days. But one in particular forever changed my life. In fact, this "one of those days" set me on a new path that led me to writing this book.

It was late spring in Butte, Montana. I will remember the date forever: June 1, 2002. The sun was shining; the temperature was a pleasant 70 degrees. The blue sky hung effortlessly over the Montana Mountains. At the time I had achieved financial freedom. I had bought and was refurbishing a beautiful old home originally built in 1906. I had the day to myself, so I decided to knock a few things off my home improvements "to do" list. I decided to first tackle putting up a picket fence by the garden. It was a simple enough project: a few saw cuts, a few screws, a couple of cuss words, and the fence was up.

Now we all know the unwritten rule about picket fences, right? They must be painted…? White, right? Exactly! So I made a quick trip to the lumberyard, bought some white paint, and came back and began painting. So I'm painting away, and as it often does so quickly in the mountains, the weather changed, and changed fast. Black clouds rolled in. All of a sudden, it didn't begin to just rain, it began to POUR, and I mean pour. So I called it a day. I gathered up all my paint supplies and threw them onto the back porch, then took the remainder of my tools down into my basement.

The basement to this house wasn't much; the floor was half cement, half dirt. It's the type of basement where you have to duck under the beams and pipes. I put my tools away, and then, because my shirt was soaked from the rain, I stripped it off. Sounds pretty mundane, right?

Here's where this story gets…interesting. What I didn't know then (five words no one ever likes to hear, right?) was that for nearly two weeks, there had been natural gas leaking into my basement. Now, natural gas is invisible—you can't see it. But you can smell it, right? *No, not when it has been filtered through dirt.* So here I am, shirtless, standing in the basement that's filled with natural gas which I can neither see nor smell.

Now, I might not have had one of "those" days except for one thing: at the time, I was a smoker. So while standing at the bottom of the stairs, I took out a cigarette, placed it in my mouth, and flicked on my lighter.

CHAPTER 2

Ka-

BOOM!

FLASH POINT

That which does not kill us makes us stronger. *
~ Friedrich Nietzsche

*And, in my case, that which did not kill me also helped me find my life's mission: to help others obtain financial freedom.

Now you know why they call me the Burnt Guy.

When I hit that lighter, BOOM: I was standing in a ball of fire. The basement literally blew up, sending a gigantic fireball out and up through the house. Have you ever been in an accident or even a near miss accident? You know, the kind where time literally slows down and your mind speeds up. For the few seconds I am standing there in this fire ball, my life is literally passing before my eyes. I know I am toast (sorry, couldn't resist). I began saying good bye to everyone I love. I mean, in all due seriousness, when was the last time you heard someone tell a story about how they blew themselves up? It's not something you often hear from the person it happened to.

Seconds later the fire goes out. But now the pain begins to set in. Have you ever burnt yourself on something scalding hot, like an iron or a stove? It hurts like hell, doesn't it? At this point, I am realizing that I am hurt *really, really, really* badly. Why? Because the pain searing across my upper body hurts like *&^%$ and my skin is beginning to fall off.

Luckily, though, I'm still coherent enough to know that I've got to get out of the basement. But I'm in bad shape. You see, while putting my tools away, I had been breathing in the gas-filled air. When I ignited the gas in the basement, the fire also ignited the gas in my lungs, burning those as well. So now I am coughing and gasping for air, barely able to breathe. I stumble upstairs but can hardly see anything because the explosion also burnt the corneas of my eyes. Somehow I make it to the top of the stairs. There I grab the metal door knob, only to immediately discover it is scorching hot. As I quickly jerk my hand back, I leave the skin of my palm hanging from the handle. While up there I also discover the door had jammed shut from the force of the explosion. I am trapped.

Now it's decision time—get out, somehow, or stay and die.

I didn't blink. Despite the excruciating pain and barely being able to see or breathe, I staggered around the basement attempting to find something to pry open the door. As I touched some of the metal tools looking for an appropriate one, the now white-hot tools burnt the palms of my hands. Luckily I found some hedge trimmers with dense Styrofoam handles I could grip. I staggered back up the stairs and began frantically trying to pry the door open. Finally, when I hit it just right, the door popped opened. I grabbed the cordless phone, called nine-one-one, and crawled out the front door to collapse on the front lawn.

My Revelation

I was life-flighted to the University of Utah Burn Center in Salt Lake City, Utah, one of the world's premier burn facilities. There I spent the next six weeks in a coma. Roughly half my body (everything from the waist up) was completely burned. After I awoke from the coma, it took me nine more months of agonizingly slow and painful rehab to learn how to do all those "little" things each of us takes for granted each day, like talking, eating, walking, and literally learning how to be comfortable in my own skin. I'm not going to spend much time here on my rehab, other than to tell you about Terrell, and how that little guy helped me find my true mission in life.

During the time I spent in Salt Lake City, I focused completely on my health—like I said; learning how to walk, talk, and so on. There was one thing during this entire time that never crossed my mind...MONEY.

Through business I had been able to semi-retire to Montana (a dream of mine). I had streams of income coming in regardless of whether I "worked" in my business or not. I had built these streams of income on purpose, with that design in mind. I just never thought it would be so life saving.

This wasn't true for anyone else I came in contact with at the Salt Lake facility. During the course of my stay in the burn unit, I not only got to meet some of the other patients, but also their families. That is, all except for this little guy named Terrell. At the time, Terrell was 18 months old. He had fallen into a campfire and had gotten badly burned. While I saw other families visit their loved ones when they could, I never saw anyone visit Terrell. One day, I finally asked a nurse about this. What she said stunned me, and helped changed the course of my life. Terrell's mom was a single mother, the nurse explained. She couldn't afford the travel expenses to come to and from Salt Lake City, and was at home working so that Terrell could have a home to come home to.

Wow, what a decision for a parent to have to make. That burn unit—talk about a frightening place to be. I know it had *me* scared spit-less. I couldn't even imagine how it must have been for Terrell. Parents, could you imagine having to make the decision between being there for your child, or working to keep your home? For the first time, I realized how unique my financial situation was. I hadn't been worrying about money, or a job, or anything like that. On the other hand, here was a mother who couldn't even be with her son when that little guy needed her the most.

I had something I could share with people, folks like Terrell's mother, folks reading this book—a roadmap, if you will, to financial freedom. And that's when it all clicked in for me, as they say. On a spiritual level, I felt like God had told me that I wasn't done yet, that my time on Earth was not going to be spent just putzing around the house and fishing and traveling. I saw then how I should go forth (O.K., I'm getting a little carried away, but you get it...) and help as many other people as possible achieve their financial targets, have freedom and choices in their lives. You see, I believe each and every one of us has something special to offer this world—gifts that were given to us to share. Most people are so trapped in their financial prison they can't give of themselves fully. One of the most rewarding things I feel blessed to do with my financial freedom and my "second chance" is to help others obtain their financial freedom so they can share their gifts and passions with this world and not make choices based on money or obligation.

Ultimately, I have come to realize this: my accident was not the greatest tragedy in my life, but rather my greatest gift.

FLASH POINT

There are no accidents—we are all here for a good reason.

CHAPTER 3

Poor Me

Little House on the Prairie

Do you remember by chance a television show back in the late 1970's/early 1980's called *Little House on the Prairie*? It was about a frontier family who faced all the various hardships, trials, and tribulations of life as a settler. Well, I HATED that flippin' show. But regardless, it did echo my childhood.

You see, if you are starting out with millions of dollars and want to become financially free, I don't know how to help you. But if you are starting out with nothing, or less than nothing, I know how to do that. Let me share with you my humble beginnings.

I grew up outside of Ellsworth, Wisconsin. Ellsworth was and still is a little town. By American standards my family was poor. I recall how we used to find a house to "rent." We would drive along gravel county roads looking for abandoned farm houses. Once we found one of these shacks, my dad would then go talk to the closest neighbor to find out who owned it. More often than not it was the neighbor. Then my dad would barter, work out a deal where we could stay for little or nothing, often using my older brother's strong back as a bargaining chip. We would stay in these "homes" until the owner would kick us out to tear down the place, or even one time to convert it into a pig barn...

which with that house didn't take much. So for the majority of my childhood we had no indoor plumbing; instead, we had a well with a hand pump and an outhouse. (I will say this, though: using an outhouse in January in Wisconsin, you do learn how to get shit done!) To heat the house we had a fuel oil burning stove set in the middle of the "living room." It would be 90 degrees in the living room, but many a night I could see my breath going up the stairs to my bedroom.

One of the reasons I grew up in poverty was my father's inability to work. One day at work my father, a factory worker, badly injured his back. The company's doctor said it was a "pulled muscle." He told my dad to go home and rest for two days, then return to work. By the second day, however, my dad could barely walk. Now, my dad was not the type to complain; he was a tough old bird. He kept saying he would "gut it out." Finally, after countless trips back and forth to the company doctor, my mom had had enough and convinced him to get another opinion. I was around nine years old at the time, but even I could tell something was wrong; when he *could* walk, my dad was crooked as a corkscrew. Immediately the other doctor took X-rays, told my dad he had a herniated disc, and scheduled him for surgery. Like anyone would do, my dad filed for workers' compensation. But the company denied his claim because the company doctor only diagnosed it as a "pulled muscle." We went eighteen months with ZERO income. You KNOW you are in a tough place when your meals consist of government surplus cheese and donations from local churches.

Don't misunderstand me, my parents were good people. They did the best they could with the knowledge they had at the time. Through our "challenges" I learned one of the most important lessons in my life, something I still carry with me today: If I wanted anything, it was up to me to get it. With this in mind, out of necessity I learned how to be an entrepreneur, one of the most important skills I possess today. One of my first businesses involved selling my Halloween candy to my classmates. I had all kinds of ventures like this.

As I grew up, I also learned something else about myself: I'm NOT what you would call a good employee. I didn't like all the little rules each employer had, so I immediately jumped right into business. I started my first business at the age of 23, and for the next eight years owned and ran a series of businesses.

My businesses became successful. However, one day it hit me that I was financially trapped. This day began like so many others, getting up, going through my morning routine.... But this particular morning I REALLY just wanted to stay home. The thought of going out and working really sucked! I tried to come up with an excuse not to go, but I kept going back to the fact that if I didn't, I wouldn't have the money coming in to pay the bills. So I dragged myself out the door.

I spent that day thinking one thought: *How did I get myself into this mess?* I was not in control of my own life. I wasn't making my own decisions anymore. I was in a FINANCIAL PRISON. I had begun my own business to gain the freedom and control in my life that I could never have had with a job. I was building a "successful" business: I had more employees, more trucks on the road, more customers, more revenue... BUT that day I also woke up to the fact I had more debt, more problems, and was working more hours than ever. And what I didn't have more of was the one thing I really wanted: FREEDOM! How did this happen?

I had bought into "the system" I had fought so hard against. *Let me know if THIS sounds familiar...*

It begins in grade school. There you learn how to work eight hours a day, five days a week. You're programmed to get up every morning and go to school, all so you can eventually get into a college to get a "good education," so that ultimately you can land a "good job" *(which I have always believed to be an oxymoron; it's like having a good heart attack)*. While continuing your education, you rack up a butt-load of student loans. In today's world it's even worse: universities and colleges are more expensive, and credit card companies target college kids.

Maybe you graduate, or not, but regardless now you're seriously in debt. You've JUST begun your financial life and you're already in the hole. (It's like starting a football game 21 points down.) Now you do what you need to do—you "get a good job." You now have money coming in; you're paying down some of the debt. Here is where you are taught to save some and invest it for retirement (401(k) account, mutual funds, etc…). Life seems good. Along the way you meet that special person and you get married and it's great, because you have combined your households and reduced your per-capita overhead. This makes you D.I.N.K.S. (dual income no kids).

Now it's time for the American Dream. You buy your first home, which puts you even more in debt. You have a mortgage, at least one car payment, and you're probably still paying student loans. Then the family starts and your expenses have grown exponentially, but you figure hey, that's what they made credit cards for.

This all seems nice…until you realize that YOU ARE NOW IN FINANCIAL PRISON. By now the novelty of your job has completely worn off, and you are at the mercy of your boss, your industry, and the economy with a family to feed, house, and clothe.

Here is when many plan their escape. They decide to "start their own business" so they do what people who start their own businesses do: they find start-up capital. Maybe that comes in the form of credit cards, a business loan (good luck), a second mortgage, or even the old let's-drain-the-life-savings (the most common, and my personal favorite).

As a new business owner, you have listened to the business news, pundits, and a few friends and family, so you know not to expect a profit for three to five years. As a result during this time you sink further and further and further into debt.

Most of these businesses WILL FAIL. These are real FACTS, folks. The businesses that do survive not only run their owners ragged, they typically put them in serious debt. Regardless, what started out as a way to free yourself slowly turns into a prison of your own creation, one which you run but are still locked up in just the same. It was at this point when I became truly irritated and open to learning the ways to creating true freedom. The only thing standing between me and freedom was the series of things I didn't know and needed to learn about money and business.

Most businesses are dependent on the economy, regulations, and the industry they are in. Whether you own a business or are an employee of a business, if you are dependent upon outside things for your success, you will end up a victim of circumstances.

What's the solution? You create your own economy!

How?

Let's find out.

CHAPTER 4

THE vs. MY Economy

There are two (actually, three) economies out there. There is **THE** economy. There is **MY** economy. And there is **YOUR** economy. It's extremely important to differentiate between these, as this is one of the core concepts that you must not only understand, but *embrace* to ultimately achieve financial freedom.

You've heard about THE economy on the evening news or on the radio; it's what you read about in newspapers and magazines. We have a plethora (big word, huh?) of experts and pundits droning on about the Gross Domestic Product (GDP), unemployment rates, Wall Street's latest ups and downs, and so on. Yes, these are important ways to measure the economy. What's important to realize, however, is that these are simply *indicators* of the economy's strength; these facts, figures, and statistics do not *control* the economy.

What does control the economy? It's simple folks: two things— FEAR and GREED, also known as "consumer confidence." It is actually something "they" try to measure.

Let's take a quick look at the past so that you can FULLY understand the truth of this statement. Back up to the 9/11 tragedy. FEAR kicks in. The government didn't want this new fear suddenly gripping the nation to take down the economy, so it falsely stimulated the economy by doing several things. One in particular worked really well: The government lowered interest rates. This spurred a buying frenzy in the housing market. And we all know about supply and demand, right? When demand goes up, what also goes up? Prices. Bingo. Housing prices began to climb.

Now generally the economy would naturally correct itself. But in this case, GREED kicked into high gear, too. People began using their homes as ATM machines, taking out second mortgages based on the assumption that their home's value would continue to appreciate. (Think gambling in Las Vegas is risky? So is betting on continued, unabated housing appreciation!) So homeowners used this money to renovate, buy toys, etc. All of this new purchasing fueled the economy even more, which caused housing prices to climb even higher! To top it off, speculators (more GREED) jumped in, buying and then quickly "flipping" (reselling) houses "betting" (rightly so, at least for a time) on housing prices shooting even higher. All seemed rosy...but this is when I got nervous. It is extremely risky to borrow "imaginary" money.

FLASH POINT

Appreciation is imaginary until you have the money in your hand!

To make matters even worse, the government and other powers that be significantly lessened the qualifications needed to obtain a mortgage. They did this for two reasons.

1. Everyone who qualified for a mortgage already HAD a mortgage!

2. Wall Street WANTED more mortgages, because they had developed a new way to bundle these into securities and sell this "product" on Wall Street.

What happened? Well, these bundled mortgage-backed securities began to sell like HOT CAKES. Why? Brokers, bankers, employers and so on considered these good, stable securities because they are made of money that has collateral, i.e., your HOUSE! (Hence the term Mortgage Backed Security you heard so much about on the news.) Remember, in its simplest terms, your mortgage is a DEBT you are obligated to pay off monthly or you lose your house. In most cases, everyone who qualifies for a mortgage typically doesn't default on their mortgage, barring a total disaster (like a spouse losing a job, etc.). Thus most people considered these bundled mortgages an extremely good, stable buy on Wall Street. In fact, they received a Triple A rating, the highest Wall Street rating a security can receive.

But again, the only way to feed the hunger of the GREED monster (which was completely out of control at this point) was to give people a loan who would not typically qualify for a mortgage, thus significantly expanding the pool, so to speak, of eligible mortgage buyers. Hence was born the sub-prime mortgage loan, which you've also heard a lot about on the news. How did the mortgage companies entice people to take out these sub-prime loans? They made it SO easy; they romanced these people with an ARM. That's right, an Adjustable Rate Mortgage, meaning that for the first couple years, the monthly mortgage payments were very reasonable, and only later would the monthly payment climb. (Some of you are now seeing where this is going; before we go there; let's go back to Wall Street.)

Wall Street, being greedy by nature, began bundling these sub-prime loans and selling them. To give credibility to this new batch of crappy bundled loans, the three main rating agencies (Moody's Investors Service Inc, Standard & Poor's Rating Services and Fitch Inc) developed a magic calculation which God himself didn't even understand. This calculation magically gave these sub-prime loan securities a "Triple A" rating as well. (Both how they did this and how they got away with it, I still don't know.) Guess what—these bundled sub-prime loan securities sold like HOT CAKES, too. But really, folks, this was like selling wolves in sheep's clothing.

Thus, we had the ingredients for a perfect storm: millions of people now receiving mortgages who, in reality, had absolutely no way to pay them. Ouch. To make matters even worse, these securities were sold aggressively on Wall Street and purchased by many retirement funds and even foreign countries. Double Ouch.

Let's fast forward a couple years. Now the ARM loan adjustments began to show up on people's mortgage bills. (And trust me; the adjustments went *up*, meaning most folk's monthly mortgage payment jumped not hundreds of dollars, but sometimes by *thousands* of dollars.) Ka-BOOM! Millions of people began defaulting on their mortgages. This led to a massive wave of foreclosures which swept across all parts of the country. With this sudden extra housing inventory, what happened to prices? They dropped like a lead balloon! Not only did the housing market take a serious dive, but so did Wall Street. People, companies, banks, etc… lost much, if not all, of their life's savings or investments. With the seeming snap of fingers, FEAR rushed in like a dark night, causing people to stop spending. Our economy, which for years had been fueled by consumer spending, screeched to a halt.

This only multiplied the problem, and our economy went down the toilet. Now you know the connection between the dots.

Some of you who followed this Greek tragedy are still wondering this: *What did AIG (the huge insurance firm) have to do with all this, and more importantly, why did they "have" to be bailed out?*

As an insurance company, AIG insured the bundled housing securities that were being sold on Wall Street (a.k.a., Credit Default Swaps). Do you see the puzzle pieces falling into place? When all the defaults and foreclosures began occurring and the value of retirement accounts began swirling down the toilet bowl, investors began flocking to AIG to claim the insurance money due to them. (It is even more interesting to note that some people took out insurance on these securities without even owning them. In other words, they were basically BETTING that this disaster would happen. Many of these folks made millions on this bet. They saw this disaster coming. Why didn't the government?)

With everyone rushing to AIG to collect their money, what happened? In short, AIG didn't have enough reserves to pay out all the claims it received. Why? One reason was that they had been too busy paying millions in bonuses to their corporate team members.

What did our government do? They stepped in to try to save your retirement account... with your money. How noble of them! This makes me SICK! How they did *not* see this coming is beyond me.

Even if you did not understand a word I just covered, here is the only thing that matters:

What could YOU have done about this?

In a word, NOTHING!

We live in a free market when times are good, and a semi-socialized market (for Wall Street) when times are bad. Sucks, doesn't it?

None of us individually could have stopped this latest economic catastrophe. So what's the solution? It's simple: you must separate YOUR economy from THE economy, and break free from your financial prison. In other words you must insure that your income is not tied directly to the economy.

This reminds of a story. I spent some time living in Butte, Montana, which happens to be an old mining town (at one time it was called the "The Richest Hill in the World"). To this day old abandoned mine shafts still surround the town. One day a couple of "old timers" went up into the hills. They happened upon an old shaft. They decided to climb down into the shaft (using rope) to try to find any gold or silver left behind. The shaft was deep, so to figure out how much rope they needed, one of them threw a rock down the shaft. They both listened intently to hear how long the rock took to hit bottom. Neither heard anything, so the second one grabbed a larger rock and repeated the process; still nothing. Then the first old timer suggested they find something even larger to throw down the shaft. Just outside the mine they stumbled upon an old railroad tie (the kind used to line the shafts). It took both of them all they had to drag that old railroad tie over and push it into the shaft. As they listened for it to hit bottom, suddenly out of nowhere a goat ran past and jumped down the shaft!! The first old timer yelled, "What was that?" They looked at each other totally perplexed, each trying to figure out why a goat would jump down the shaft. Seconds later a frantic farmer ran up to them and asked them if they had seen a goat! The second old timer pointed down the black hole and said, "Yes, as a matter of fact, one just ran by and jumped down the shaft!" The farmer scratched his head and said, "It couldn't have been my goat 'cause I had him tied to an old railroad tie."

The moral of the story is this: *Be careful what you are tied to!* If you're tied to the economy and it gets thrown down a shaft (which it has and does on a regular basis), you go down with it.

Your Economy

Let's take a look at **YOUR** economy. I realize this must feel strange to you. In fact, this may be the first time you have ever examined your life and financial situation quite like this.

Honestly, how is YOUR economy? How are you doing financially? Are you prepared for your future, your retirement, and the kids' college funds? Or, are you spiraling further and further into debt? Or maybe you're a slave to your job or business with no exit plan. Maybe you spent years giving your money to some clown in a suit who lost it all. Is a little financial freedom on the menu? To move forward toward your targets, it's extremely important to get really clear regarding your current financial situation. (We will look at this in more detail a little later in the book, and we do this in-depth in our Catch Fire University curriculum.)

My Economy

Financial freedom is possible. You see, I have separated (untied) "MY" Economy from THE Economy. My personal economy happens to be booming. Not bragging here, just stating a fact. I am not tied to nor fall victim to the swings of "THE" Economy (the marketplace, trends, stupid government, corporate regulation or de-regulations, and so on).

I have done the work so that money comes in weekly and monthly whether I get out of bed or not. I have peace of mind, complete freedom, and a lot of time to do research for this book!

I also like to think of MY economy as holistic, meaning I have several *currencies* in my economy; yes, I have money and finances, but also relationships, my health, giving, and so on. You have all heard that money won't make you happy. No, it won't, but it sure helps!

FLASH POINT

There is only one thing worse than being rich and miserable, and that is being broke and miserable.

We all have many human needs aching to be filled. Money makes meeting *all* of these needs *so* much easier. Think about the economy of relationships. How would that economy rate if you had all the time in the world to spend with your parents, spouse, or children? (Or maybe enough money to escape them!)

It's my gift to you to be able to share with you how to do this. Before we move on to achieving financial freedom, it is vitally important to spend some time examining our current financial institutions and de-bunking many of the myths associated with the money game "rules" taught to us (incorrectly) since we were infants. If we don't know WHY the things we do and have been taught don't work, it will be much more difficult to change them. Understanding and awareness are the first elements of real change.

To create a solution you must first be aware of the problem, so get ready to be irritated as I expose the smoke and mirrors!

FLASH POINT

It is no longer a matter of "the haves" and the "have-nots"; it's a matter of the informed and uninformed!

PART 2

The Problem

CHAPTER 5

Myth Busting

Most of us have heard of the show "Myth Busters" where a couple of guys take common myths and put them to the test. They see if they are plausible, or, if not, they "bust" them. So let's take a look at a few commonly held financial myths and put them to the test. Please note that as I examine these, I will assume that the desired outcome is financial freedom, or at least being financially well off.

MYTH #1: Get a Good Education, Get a Job.

I know that most people will say they don't believe this anymore, but what people say doesn't determine what they believe; what they do, on the other hand, definitely does indicate their beliefs. Most Americans have jobs, so most people subscribe to this myth.

Back in the days of defined benefit pensions, this was plausible. You could get a job for a large company (like General Motors), work at the company for 30 or 40 years, and then retire with a great pension. You achieved Financial Freedom for your golden years. Does this still hold true today? No! Defined benefit pensions today are as rare as an albino spotted owl. Large companies have passed the responsibility of retirement onto the employee using the ole 401(k) trick. Yes, that's right—the 401(k) was designed to help big business, not you. I'll talk more about this a bit later. To really see if this myth is plausible or not, you simply have to look at the results: Most statistics show that about 95 percent of employees will NEVER be financially free in their desired life style.

I have never been able to make a connection between formal education and financial freedom, but I can connect formal education to financial prison. Most formal education teaches us to be a higher-level employee. In other words, just broke at a higher level, with no hope of retirement or financial freedom.

As far as the good job part, I find that to be an oxymoron. Let's look at what a "good job" does for us. It tells us where to be and for how long, along with what we will be doing when we are there. We generally get paid way less than we are worth, and as soon as we stop giving it our time and life energy, the pay stops (ensuring we are never financially free). On the other hand, as soon it makes sense for the company to get rid of you, THEY WILL. If you want to be free in this lifetime and you have a job, you must make an escape plan. This is one of the things we teach in our Catch Fire University.

So, this myth is seriously BUSTED!

If you follow this myth, you will probably end up financially BUSTED.

MYTH #2: My 401(k) Will Take Care of My Retirement!

This Ponzi scheme (can ya tell I'm not a fan?) makes Bernie Madoff look like a measly shoplifter. First, let's be clear: the real reason for the 401(k) is for large companies, Wall Street, and the government to gain.

Let's look at what the 401(k) does for large companies. Basically, it replaced the old defined benefit pension (where the company gave you a guaranteed amount of money in retirement until you die) with a much less costly employee benefit. In their zeal to cut costs and compete with Japan and other foreign companies in the 70's and 80's, corporations starting promoting the 401(k) along with the tax advantages. Throwing in an employee's ability to purchase certain stock made this oh-so tempting.

Wall Street

Oh, let's talk about that bastion of greed. The 401(k) represented the perfect storm in terms of getting America to hand over money so the Wall Street big boys could continue to play their games. What most workers don't know is that fees, rebates, and revenue-sharing agreements (among employers, 401(k) administrators and mutual funds—of course, all this is buried in the fine print or not disclosed at all) are stealing their nest eggs. The U.S. Department of Labor lists 17 distinct 401(k) fees, including ones for record keeping, legal services, and toll-free telephone numbers.

The most common fees 401(k) fees:

a) Management fees
b) Administrative fees
c) Distribution fees (the top three usually averaging about 1 percent a year)
d) Sales loads (often averaging 1.4 percent a year)
e) Trading costs (averaging .5-1 percent in an actively managed fund)
f) Excess capital gains taxes when a portfolio is turned over

Of course, this isn't anywhere close to being a complete list.

*"More and more Americans are relying on 401(k) plans
to provide their retirement income. In spite of that, there
are few requirements for fund managers to tell participants
how much they are paying in fees."*
- Senator Herb Kohl (D-WI)

But Doug, the stock market makes a 7 percent return over time. We have all heard that one. But consider this: the bulk of those gains happened during a 20-year span, and is no indication as to the future. Matter of fact, that span was when companies, and Wall Street, as well as our government, were twisting our arm to give our money to Wall Street. Couple that along with the baby boom bubble and yes, you will have a period of substantial growth that bumps the average up to 7-8 percent. That's like having a room of 10 people, one being Bill Gates, and then saying the average income of the room is in the billions. If we look at historic data, we will find that the 20 years after major corrections in the market the average is between 1-2 percent gains, which will get eaten up by fees (because you call that toll free number so much). And let's not forget those billions of dollars of bonus money for those "salt of the earth" CEO's.

As far as I can tell, we still have a supply and demand economy, so my question is this: When all these baby boomers retire and start to sell off to fund their retirement and flood the market, aren't stocks and mutual fund prices going to go down?

But Doug, what about my employer's matching contributions? That's a great deal, right? Yes, for your employer. But let's be honest—it's not a match!!!! Rather than pay you the money as salary, they instead match your contribution and get a big old tax break. Again, the 401(k) was designed to help big business, not you. Anyway, the employer match is becoming a thing of the past as well. In fact, with this recession, companies are abandoning the match completely, leaving you on your own.

"The 401(k) will turn out to be the greatest systemic financial hoax ever perpetrated on an unsuspecting public."
- William Wollman, The Great 401(k) Hoax

But Doug, my 401(k) gives me a big tax break. No, you don't get a break; you get a tax increase on your invested money. Why? The standard 401(k)s are tax deferred, not tax free (big difference).

FLASH POINT

Tax deferred does not mean tax free.

Simply put, this means that you don't pay taxes when you put the money into the account, but you are taxed when the money comes out. Think about this: in the future, with our country already $50 trillion in debt (if you include Social Security and Medicaid), do you think taxes will be lower than they are now, the same, or higher? You got it—higher. So our government has figured out how to tax current earnings at a future (higher) rate. Flippin brilliant! I have had some fund managers say that they tell their clients they will be in a lower tax bracket when they retire, so the 401(k) is a good deal. Even after they tell their clients it doesn't work, do people still give them their money? Yes! Insane!! I know I don't invest to have my income go down, do you?

This myth is BUSTED!

FLASH POINT

The 401(k) is the gun used in the mugging of America.

I have met a lot of financially free people in my life, and not a one has done it through a 401(k). If you have nothing else but a full match by your employer, fine, but start looking for something else, too.

MYTH #3: Social Security Will Be Sound For Many Years To Come!

First off, I can't figure out why they call it Social Security; it's not enough to allow you to be social, and it sure as hell isn't secure.

Social Security is a "pay-as-you-go" scheme. This means that while you're working now, the government is taking the money you are putting into the system and giving it to current Social Security recipients who are, of course, no longer working. In order to get workers to accept this system, the government promises that in the future, when it's your turn to retire, they'll take other people's money and give it to you. Think of Social Security as a government version of Bernie Madoff's giant Ponzi scheme.

As long as a lot of people die before collecting any benefits, or die without collecting a lot of benefits, the system works. In 1950, the worker-to-beneficiary ratio was 16.5-to-1, meaning 16.5 people were working and paying in to the system for every one person collecting benefits. With people living longer, however, the worker-to-beneficiary ratio has fallen dramatically, to 3.1-to-1. What's more, within 20 years, this is expected to drop to 2.1-to-1. Because of this falling ratio, over the years the government has raised tax rates, and now must consider further adjustments.

Few people working today understand the tax burden of the Social Security system. On their paychecks, those employed see that 6.2 percent of their gross pay goes to pay for Social Security. What they don't see is that employers match this tax payment with an equal 6.2 percent payment. Now on the surface it may seem that employers are paying half of the Social Security taxes, but that's not the case. Even though the employers are legally obligated to pay, they just make up the difference in lower wages. So workers really are shouldering 12.4 percent of their income as part of the Social Security tax burden, it's just that half of this burden is hidden from the workers. Kind of slick, isn't it?

Now to address the common belief that SSI is running a surplus, the answer to that question is yes and no. Yes, there has been a running surplus of money from Social Security for a long time, so somewhere there is a large warehouse of money with a sign above the door saying "SSI SURPLUS MONEY FOR FUTURE RECIPIENTS – DO NOT TOUCH". Yep, and pigs fly, too. In reality, *our government has already spent this surplus money* and replaced it with government bonds. These bonds are nothing more then pieces of paper stating that U.S. taxpayers owe this money. Go ahead; shake your head, read it again if you have to. Our government has a term for this. It's called 'intra-governmental lending.' This is like taking money out of your Savings account, replacing it with an IOU, putting it in your Checking account, spending it, and telling everyone it is still in your Savings account. So our government is borrowing money from itself. Don't try this at home, folks—the fat cats within our government are professionals. But wait, there is more; as the worker-to-recipient ratio gets worse, the $2.4 trillion of bonds in the Trust Fund represent Social Security revenues *that need to be collected a second time*. Why? Because the tax revenues did not go towards Social Security spending when they were initially collected; in fact, I am not sure anyone knows where it all went. The bottom line is this: all of the intra-governmental debt represents future higher taxes for you and me.

The interest on the bonds in the Trust Fund is another issue. In 2008, the Social Security Administration (SSA) racked up $116 billion of interest payments on its $2.4 trillion of bonds, interest payments that were made in the form of more Treasury bonds for the Trust Fund. (Basically the government is paying IOU's with IOU's.) The government loans itself money and then issues bonds to pay itself interest on that lending. This is not an insignificant amount. In the last ten years, the SSA has collected $754 billion of interest on its share of the intra-governmental debt. The Trustees Report declares that, starting in 2016, the "deficits will be made up by redeeming trust fund assets until reserves are exhausted in 2037." This is sleight of hand. The actual day of reckoning is 2016, not 2037. By 2037, the Trust Fund will be depleted. But the Trust Fund is irrelevant. Regardless of the status of the Trust Fund, if the current estimates are correct, beginning in 2016, the system will need significant additional tax revenues.

Bottom line, only higher taxes and reduced benefits will save this program.

This myth is sooo **BUSTED!**

I wouldn't count on the Social Security Administration for anything in the future.

Final Thoughts

Now that you understand that the common strategies to create "financial security" are not only flawed but flat out don't work, I am sure you want to dive in, learn more about how to achieve your own financial freedom. We're getting very close to that, I promise. For now, though, it's critically important for you to learn more about how our systems work. If you do not know the rules to a game or the main target of the game, you can never win. The vast majority of Americans do not know the rules to the financial and economic games our country operates by…which is part of the reason they are broke and up-to-their-eyeballs in debt. Keep reading and you will become more educated and informed than 95 percent of the people you know.

CHAPTER 6

The Three Hands in Your Pocket

Why is it so difficult to get ahead financially these days? Why does it seem like, even with our increased standard of living, most people today seem to be doing WORSE than their parents did 20 or 30 years ago? Some of you may remember when many households had just one bread winner (if not, most have seen re-runs of *Leave it to Beaver*). Back in the 40's, 50's and 60's, most middle class Americans had a single wage earner. Now, of course, most households are dual income, with both working 40 to 50 hour weeks while the PlayStation and X-Box raise the children. If you listen to the financial pundits, we are richer than ever as our economy has grown leaps and bounds since the 50's. If this is true, who stole all the money?

Prosperity has been robbed by three main culprits. I like to call these the three hands in your pockets. They are:

1. Taxes

2. Inflation

3. Debt

All three of these hands are intertwined.

Taxes

Taxes to me are a good idea gone bad. The idea of pooling money together to cover shared expenses is great; this means you don't have to go out and build your own roads to drive to work. Yes, city and state governments as well as the federal government need money to operate, and provide us needed services like police and fire protection, good roads, etc. But folks, we are taxed to death! Don't believe me, check this out.

Daniel Mitchell of The Heritage Foundation says this: "According to data from the Internal Revenue Service, the top 1 percent of income earners pay nearly 35 percent of the **income tax** burden; the top 10 percent pay 65 percent; and the top 25 percent pay nearly 83 percent. The bottom 50 percent of income earners, on the other hand, pays barely 4 percent of income taxes." Considering that the majority of America's population is in the bottom 50 % of earners, high income earners, seemed to be *disproportionally penalized* when it comes to paying taxes.

The other miscellaneous taxes also add up. Check out this chart:

How Much Tax Do We Really Pay?

Item	Rate	Notes
Federal personal income tax	17%	Top 25% rate. It ranges from a credit up to well over 40%.
State & local income taxes	10.1%	State taxes range from under 6% to over 12%. Local taxes run from zero to 2.75%.
Sales tax	8.6%	Figure is the average rate. State sales taxes range up to 7% and local taxes run from zero to over 5%.
Social security & Medicaid	7.65%	Total rate is actually 15.3% since half is paid by the employer, but we're ignoring that to be kind
Federal corporate income tax share	3%	Based on corporate taxes being approximately 1/6 of personal taxes, and that they are paid by individuals in the final analysis.

Property tax	2.5%	Yearly average actual costs range from under $200 in Alaska to almost $1900 in New Jersey.
Fuel/gasoline tax	.5%	Approximately 23% of the 2005 gasoline price is for federal & state taxes. The federal excise tax is 18.4 cents per gallon. Per the CPI, about 6% of the average budget is for transportation. Estimated.
Other	.5%	Estimated.

Total tax percentage paid by the above average U.S. citizen, 2005:
54.4%

Note 1: **the total tax paid is closer to 46-48%, since the figures above do not distinguish between taxes on gross and net income.** Note also that the Tax Foundation's numbers are closer to 34% for the actual "average" US citizen.

Note 2: Inflation effects are likely quite understated - if actual inflation is 6% and one is only earning 4%, the tax rate is not the main issue.

Note 3: This page is not intended to be definitive and completely accurate on tax rates and issues - to do so would be virtually impossible considering all the factors. It is primarily intended to show a fuller picture than is normally presented.

Still not convinced that Americans pay a lot of taxes? Check out this PARTIAL list of taxes imposed on U.S. citizens:

- Accounts Receivable Tax
- Building Permit Tax
- Capital Gains Tax
- CDL license Tax
- Cigarette Tax

- Corporate Income Tax
- Court Fines (indirect taxes)
- Deficit spending
- Dog License Tax
- Federal Income Tax
- Federal Unemployment Tax (FUTA)
- Fishing License Tax
- Food License Tax
- Fuel permit tax
- Gasoline Tax
- Hunting License Tax
- Inflation
- Inheritance Tax Interest expense (tax on the money)
- Inventory tax IRS Interest Charges (tax on top of tax)
- IRS Penalties (tax on top of tax)
- Liquor Tax
- Local Income Tax
- Luxury Taxes
- Marriage License Tax
- Medicare Tax
- Property Tax
- Real Estate Tax
- Septic Permit Tax
- Service Charge Taxes
- Social Security Tax

- Road Usage Taxes (Truckers)
- Sales Taxes
- Recreational Vehicle Tax
- Road Toll Booth Taxes
- School Tax
- State Income Tax
- State Unemployment Tax (SUTA)
- Telephone federal excise tax
- Telephone federal universal service fee tax
- Telephone federal, state and local surcharge taxes
- Telephone minimum usage surcharge tax
- Telephone recurring and non-recurring charges tax
- Telephone state and local tax
- Telephone usage charge tax
- Toll Bridge Taxes
- Toll Tunnel Taxes
- Traffic Fines (indirect taxation)
- Trailer Registration Tax
- Utility Taxes
- Vehicle License Registration Tax
- Vehicle Sales Tax
- Watercraft Registration Tax
- Well Permit Tax
- Workers Compensation Tax

What the lawyers make us say (disclaimer): The above is presented for educational and/or entertainment purposes only. Under no circumstances should it be mistaken for professional investment advice, nor is it at all intended to be taken as such. The commentary and other contents simply reflect the opinion of the authors alone on the current and future status of the markets and various economies. It is subject to error and change without notice.

Whew, kind of makes your head spin, doesn't it? I know it does mine! Again, this near-constant contribution we make through taxes significantly limits what we get to keep of the money we earn. Your ability to **limit your exposure** to taxes is paramount to becoming free. I am NOT a tax expert, but a bit later you are going to get some tips from one of the best in the world (stay tuned).

While politicians continually argue about who should pay more taxes, the real question is never addressed: "Where in the hell does all our money go?" Does it go to bail out companies deemed "too big to fail"? Since when is that possible in a capitalist system?

Our tax money also funds programs that give hand outs, which simply perpetuates itself. The most ironic thing I have witnessed in a long time was during the health care debate. We had politicians opposing taxpayer dollars being spent on health insurance, yet these same politicians currently enjoy health insurance provided by your taxpayer dollars!! Here's my point: because the system is crazy, the best steward of your money is YOU! If you ever want out of the mayhem, then you need to learn the rules so you don't give your money to people who don't know what they are doing. We teach proven and legal strategies to reduce your tax exposure in our Catch Fire University.

Inflation

I consider inflation the second hand in your pocket, and the sneakiest. Most believe inflation occurs when the price for products goes up. This isn't inflation folks, rising prices are a *symptom* of inflation.

Inflation can happen for many reasons, and can happen in specific markets; demand can exceed supply causing prices to rise. Increased cost of production can also cause inflation; for example when there is a hard freeze in Florida and the prices of oranges goes up.

The inflation I am talking about occurs when too much money pursues various goods and services. What I mean is this: when an excess of money pursues goods and services, it causes the prices of those goods and services to rise. Now notice, I said "price"—I didn't say *value*.

Let me use an analogy to help explain. Say I'm on a deserted island with two other people. One guy has an apple. I'm the only one with any money and all I have is $5. Assuming he would sell it, what do you think the guy with the apple would be willing to sell it for? Five bucks, right? Right. Suddenly the third person realizes he has a $20 bill stuffed away in his pocket. What do you think the price of the apple would be now? Yes, $20.

The price of the apple increased. But did the apple change at all? No. Did its *value* go up? No again. Whether one person (me) was going to pay five bucks for it, or the other guy, who was going to pay $20, the apple was the same, but it went up in price. It's called 'perceived value'. Why? Because there was more money on the island. Right now in the U.S. (our island), there is more money in circulation then ever before, and they seem to keep printing more and more. This is a BIG reason why your grocery bill, gas bill, and electric bills keep going up.

What has been happening in the United States for years (primarily since the Nixon administration in the early 1970's when we left the gold standard) is this: more and more money has been printed and gone into our economy (the supply). This has caused prices to rise (inflation). Thus, what used to cost you X now costs you X+.

A BRIEF but IMPORTANT History Lesson:

The GOLD STANDARD

It used to be that EVERY American dollar printed HAD to be backed by a set amount of gold stored in the government's reserve. The government could not print money unless there was that gold guarantee. SMART business. We were one of MANY countries operating this way. This type of system has been used by all kinds of cultures since 700 AD.

Things officially changed on August 15, 1971. President Nixon decided to *kybosh* the gold standard, which was officially established in the U.S. in 1873. His decision truly was the beginning of this financial chaos we are in today. Now the government and Federal Reserve simply print money out of thin air—money backed by nothing but a "commitment by the American taxpayer to make good on it."

I know what some of you are thinking: well, inflation is just the way economies work, it's always been that way. NO! NO! NO! NO! You may be shocked to learn that from the 1670's until 1940, the ONLY time we experienced inflation was when we were at war *(because war causes deficit spending)!*

> **Deficit spending** is the amount by which a government, private company, or individual's spending exceeds income over a particular period of time. It is also called a "deficit" or "budget deficit."
>
> It's the opposite of a budget surplus. It is spending *without* a return on investment.

The cost of living **always** returned to its previous levels after the war. So for THREE HUNDRED years a dollar was a dollar! During the 1940's (during World War II), however, we started to find loopholes. We strayed from the gold standard and simply printed money (Fiat Money). Plus we never dismantled the war machine. From a purely monetary standpoint, there is no positive return on investment in building a bomb!

> The term **fiat money** is used to mean:
>
> - any money declared by a government to be legal tender
>
> - state-issued money which is neither legally convertible to any other thing, nor fixed in value in terms of any objective standard

To further explain inflation, I am going to reference back to our current situation. The "bailout" of the institutions that ran our economy into a ditch must be PAID for somehow! The bailout has and will continue to be paid for by putting a lot more money (fiat money) into circulation (not to mention all of the deficit spending occurring as we pay for two wars). This is going to flood our system with *trillions* of Fiat dollars; a.*k.a.*, *more money on the island.*

> ### FLASH POINT
>
> *Inflation occurs when too much money pursues goods and services.*

To give you some staggering numbers and charts on inflation, here is an article written about the subject by my friend, Simon Cornelius. Simon is originally from England so if you can, read this with an English accent.

Today is April 13, 2010; the stock market is rising—whoopee! My investments are going up in value, which means I'm making money. I have been investing in the stock market for decades and over time, my portfolio value has grown. To most this would be good news. Even if I had bought into the stock market at its height in 2000, and sold at the height in 2007, my portfolio still increased and I made a killing, right?

WRONG, WRONG, and WRONG!

One of the common misconceptions people have is that if the value of their portfolio went up due to increases in the stock market, if they were to cash it out, they would be able to buy more "stuff" than they could when they initially invested their money.

What they fail to understand is the effects of inflation eroding their buying power. Here's a sobering way of looking at it using the official CPI (Consumer Price Index) which is produced by the Bureau of Labor Statistics. The CPI measures how many dollars it takes to buy the same amount of "stuff" (food, shelter, etc.) each month, and is the standard way of measuring inflation. We'll be conservative here, since the CPI has been bastardized over the years, and cheaper items are substituted from time to time to mask the true effects of inflation. For example, the BLS used to price steak, but then substituted for hamburger meat or chicken. So a basket of goods purchased in 1913 is NOT the same basket of goods purchased in 2010. Anyway, I digress, and we'll use the official CPI numbers to see how much buying power you would really have over the years.

If you had one share of the DJIA index and cashed it out, (assuming no fees or taxes) how much "stuff" (as measured by the CPI) could you buy?

Between 1965 and 1982, even though the stock market went up, your buying power went **down**. Kind of like a "silent recession."

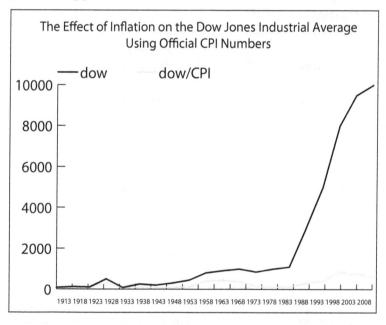

Even though the stock market was higher in 2007 than in 2000, in real purchasing power, we still have a way to go to have as much purchasing power today as we did in 2000.

In other words, inflation is quietly eating away your hard earned money.

It's a mistake to look at your worth in terms of dollars, but instead how much "stuff" can you buy.

Let's take a look at gasoline and see if you're able to buy more gas in a rising stock market. After all, we're a nation of gas guzzlers. A gallon of gas cost between $.85 to $1.40 from 1980 to 1996. Pretty consistent, wouldn't you agree? Then we know what happened next! $4 for a gallon of gas. Will we ever see gas for a buck again?

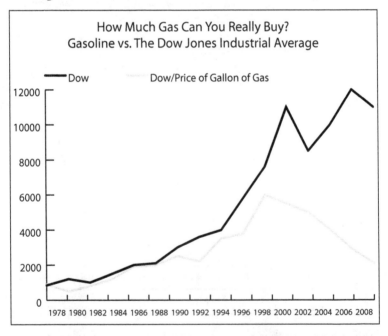

So let's see how many gallons of gas could be bought for one share of the DJIA index.

As expected, as the stock market increased and gasoline stayed relatively unchanged, you could buy more and more gas with your share of the DJIA.

But, in 2010, you can only buy as much gas as you could in the early 1990's. In fact, since 1998, you've been able to buy less and less gasoline with your share of the DJIA. Your real purchasing power has declined. A picture is worth a thousand words!

The same thing can be done for non-food items like dishwashers, cars, TVs etc. This ain't your grandfather's dollar anymore.

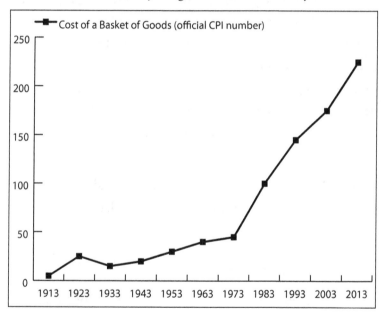

Resources:

Gasoline prices: US Energy Information Association: www.eia.doe.gov

CPI: Bureau of Labor Statistics www.bls.gov

Accessed; March 28, 2010

Hey, it's Doug again. If you fully understand what was explained in this last section on inflation, you probably just broke out in a sweat. I don't own a crystal ball, but I can see some writing on the wall: Inflation, if not hyperinflation, is on the way. What this means is that the PRICE of goods and services will continue to rise *even though their value remains the same.* Life may drastically change in the next 20 years if we do not return to some commonsense business practices. (It hasn't helped that our current leader, President Obama, has NO business experience, while his predecessor, President Bush, ran every business he ever owned into the ground.)

I hear you asking this question: What the hell do I do? Understand, if hyperinflation hits, cash is no longer king. That $5,000 you have in a coffee can buried in the back yard may or may not buy a loaf of bread. Let's go back to the apple analogy. In inflationary times, which position would you rather be in: the person with the money trying to buy some apples, or the guy with the apples? It's probably a good idea to own some of those "apples."

While I'm not here to give you investment advice, I strongly advise you do three things to hedge against inflation:

1. OWN some "apples"

2. Own your own Business

3. Learn how to live within (and ideally BELOW) your means

You see, when the cost of everything goes up and you're *already* strapped and living paycheck to paycheck, you are in SERIOUS trouble! With no room between your earnings and your expenses, you will experience a radical shift in your lifestyle. Living *below* your means creates the room, or buffer, needed when the whiff of inflation is in the air. Getting your financial house IN ORDER becomes even more crucial. (Note: you'll learn about cutting overhead later in this book and in our Catch Fire University.)

Debt

> **Debt:** Something owed, such as money, goods, or services. An obligation or liability to pay or render something to someone else.
>
> **However debt in the true accounting sense** is when you have more liabilities than assets. And assets meaning those things that provide income or potential cash flow in our lives.

Debt is the third and most lethal of the three hands in your pocket. I want to be crystal clear about this: debt is the enemy to financial freedom, period, over and out. I hear all this talk about "good debt." Good debt? Some people say that if you borrow money at a low rate, and turn around and make money at a higher rate, that it is good debt. Say you take out a loan to buy a house and then you rent the house and it covers the mortgage plus puts a few dollars in your pocket. I call this **investing,** not good debt.

Rule of thumb: if it does not put money in your pocket, it's DEBT.

FLASH POINT

*Debt occurs when you spend your financial future
for immediate gratification.*

Why and how has debt become a way of life in America? We have mortgages, car loans, credit cards; we can finance just about anything, which is the way it's always been, right? No. Prior to the 1970's there wasn't a lot of consumer debt. For example, take credit card debt. In 1967, U.S. consumers had about $1.4 billion of credit card debt. Flash forward to 2007: now U.S. consumers hold $972 billion of credit card debt.

The Debt Nation

To understand the problems associated with debt, we must first understand the relationship between debt and money. Let's get one thing straight first: every U.S. dollar created since we left the gold standard is "debted", or loaned, into existence. Crazy, isn't it?

In a very simplified version, here's what takes place:

- ➲ Our government issues a bond (a piece of paper which basically promises that taxpayers will re-pay you for the amount stated).

- ➲ This is sold on the market.

- ➲ Many of these are bought by the Federal Reserve.

- ➲ With help of the U.S Treasury, the Federal Reserve then converts these bonds into dollars. They print money, so to speak.

- ➲ This money is lent out to our banks.

Keep in mind that the Federal Reserve is not—I repeat, not—a government agency. It is neither a reserve of money or run by the Federal government. Rather, it is a conglomerate (group) of banks and investment firms, and their CEO's. And the only thing backing the money is a promise that U.S. taxpayers will make good on the money.

The National Debt

Let's talk too about our national debt. As of March 6, 2006, the national debt stands at $8.2 trillion. That's TRILLION, folks. The American taxpayers paid the Federal Reserve banking system $173,875,979,369.66 in interest on that debt in just five short months, from October, 2005, through February, 2006. In a few short years, our national debt has risen to $10.7 trillion. With the recent economic meltdown, the national debt will have risen even more dramatically. And guess what—it will continue to go up. The United States will never even be able to repay *the interest on the loan*, let alone the principal.

Because of this debt, in actuality the Federal Reserve "owns" the United States. Because of this ownership, our elected officials are beholden to the bankers who are shareholders in the FED, not the American people. No one, not Congress, not the president, dares to oppose the FED; because it controls the money supply, it is all-powerful. No con artist or group of con artists in history has ever perpetrated a scam that even approaches the scope of this one, folks!

Henry Ford once said, "It is well enough that people of the nation do not understand our banking and monetary system, for if they did, I believe there would be a revolution before tomorrow morning." How true!

NOTE: To all Canadians, Australians, residents of the UK, and any industrialized nation.

The systems described in this book are the U.S. systems; however they are also applicable to YOU.

Decades ago we entered into a global system. What happens here in the U.S. affects what happens in the rest of the world's nations. Being an informed global citizen is important to the success of your Financial Life!

It would also be naïve at best to think that your health care costs, taxes, and inflation aren't affecting you. And if you or your Government is accumulating debt, and if you use a Bank, these sections will all be very applicable to you.

Fractured Reserve Banking System

At this point the money begins to be lent out to Americans everywhere who are buying a home or a new car, who need a line of credit, etc. I call this the GREAT MONEY CREATING FACTORY. It is the biggest money scam ever imagined, and I will show you why right now.

As you are about to see, the real purpose of the banking system is to create money, and they use a legal system, (*the fractured reserve banking system*) to do so.

Here is how it works:

➲ You deposit **$100,000** into your bank account.

➲ While the bank holds your money, it must keep a fraction of it in reserve (between 3 and 10%.) For this, example let's use 10%.

➲ Thus, $10,000 is held in reserve.

➲ What does the bank do with the other $90,000? They can loan that money out.

Here's where it gets interesting. The $90,000 loaned out by the bank shows as an **asset** on their balance sheet, which means the bank can loan out 90% of the asset's value, or, in this case, $81,000.

Press "pause" for a moment and shake your head—you got it! The bank just made money out of thin air! Maybe you already see what's coming: that $81,000 also shows up as an asset in their books, therefore they can loan out 90% of that, which is $72,900. The bank can do this upwards of SIX times according our laws.

But just look at three times: The bank turned the ORIGINAL $100,000 (which wasn't theirs to begin with) into **$243,900** flooding into our system, and the only thing backing these dollars is our commitment as taxpayers to make it good on it.

What would happen if everyone wanted to pull out their deposits? The banks couldn't cover this, and they would collapse!

Now what would happen if everyone paid off all of their debt? There would be NO money in circulation. Why? Because it is all imaginary money that has been "debted" into existence!

Here's the kicker, folks: *Our whole system has been built on YOU and everyone else being in debt.* Our tax laws promote it; our fiscal policy insures it; and almost every politician will do everything he or she can to keep it going. No, Doug not my congressman! Think about the how the Bush Administration GAVE the banks $700 billion dollars (TARP) to make sure they would stay afloat and continue to loan money. Why didn't we just help folks pay their mortgage, which would have given the banks their money back so they could loan it out again? Because that would not have been NEARLY as profitable to the banks! Understand, there are two lobbyists from the financial services sector for every one congressman. The Secretary of the Treasury and the Federal Reserve Chair *all* come from the banking industry, and all of their friends are still in the business. Even if you're reading this book 10 years from when I am writing it now, this will still be true. It's the system, and every system is designed to perpetuate itself.

The Personal Cost

Now that we understand who ends up paying for our country's debt (taxpayers), let's take a look at the cost of personal consumer debt. (Every debt you have is spending your future; this includes mortgages, car payments, credit cards, etc.)

> ## FLASH POINT
>
> *Taking on DEBT is a bet you place on yourself that you will make more in the future than you are making currently.*

If you do actually make more, you will probably be O.K. But what happens if your income decreases, or you lose your job, or inflation causes your living expenses to go through the roof, or you rack up more debt than your income has increased? You end up in serious trouble.

More than 60 percent of Americans have fallen into serious debt. When you are paying on this burden, creating financial freedom is almost impossible. To create true financial freedom, you must become debt-free.

Credit Card Debt

You may be surprised to learn that when you purchase something with a credit card, in a lot of cases the credit card bank behind it will make more profit from that sale than the merchant who sold you the physical product. Go ahead, read that line again.

Say you have $15,000 of credit card debt at 18% interest (which, unbelievably, is a little low). If only paying the minimum payment due each month, it would take you more than 31 years to pay off the debt, during which time you will have paid $21,924.72 in interest. Oh, and if you're ever late on a payment or if you go beyond your limit, the fees and penalties start. Then interest is charged on the fees and penalties along with the principal, and it snowballs to the point you can't keep up. According to Steve Bucci, president of Money Management International Financial Education Foundation, the average person carries 11 "credit vehicles". Most people have between five and 10 credit cards, and the average U.S. household carries more than $9,000 dollars of credit card debt. That's the flippin' *average* of just credit card debt.

Car Loan

Let's take a look at car loans. Say you purchase a $30,000 car at 8% interest for 60 months. You will pay more than **$9,000 of interest alone**! You literally just gave away $9,000 of your future earnings. (Plus you lose thousands of dollars the second you drive the new car off the lot in terms of depreciation.) But Doug, you say, I need a car. How am I supposed to get around? Again, if Freedom is the target, is the Cadillac Escalade necessary right now? Or, can you down grade *(FOR NOW)* until you get out of the Financial Prison that is "our system."

Dream or Trap

Now let's take a look at something as wholesome as apple pie—yes, the American dream of owning a home! We have been taught that you really haven't arrived until you own a home. And this home will be the largest "investment" we will ever make. BULLSHIT! That's right—we are taught these things by the industries that get rich off the housing market. These, of course, include the banks and boy, oh boy, do they make a killing off it.

Put me on the record here: Your home is not an investment, it is a debt! It costs you money! It's not just the mortgage; you also must pay insurance, taxes, H.O.A. fees, repairs, and maintenance. But Doug, you say, my house went up in value since I bought it (I don't hear that much anymore). So you sell this house and then what do you do? You buy another house in the same market. The only ones making money off this transaction are the banks and your realtor. I will have people argue with me about this, and they are usually the ones with the most debt!

Don't misunderstand me—I'm not against owning a home! However, I do advocate knowing the total cost of home ownership up front, and making sure that this is **within your means**! If looking at what happened in 2008 doesn't convince you of that, no one can help you.

Let's look at some numbers of what the American dream really costs. It starts with loan fees, which they like to call closing costs, inspections, document fees, and so on. Let's say $4,000. Next, let's use a lowball figure for upkeep and general maintenance, say, $1 per square ft. per year. For this example, we'll use a 2,000-square-foot home, making your annual maintenance bill about $2,000. With a mortgage of $300,000 on a 30-year term, fixed at 6%, your total cost over the course of the loan will be $647,514.57, of which **$347,514.57 was INTEREST**. During those 30 years, we will have at least $60,000 in maintenance, conservatively $135,000 in taxes, and $60,000 in insurance. Home Owner Association (HOA) fees will add another $10,000, upgrades another $75,000 (which you took out a second mortgage to pay for), and $10,000 in miscellaneous expenses. All of this adds up to

$1,001,514.57 of your future earnings you committed simply for the privilege of living in your own home.

Fast forward to the end of your 30 year term; now you can sell your house and make money, right? Sure, you may get your $1 million back, but then where are you going to live? Under a bridge? Probably not; more than likely you will turn around and buy again in the **same market** and start all over again. Please realize that this is *exactly* what the system *wants* you to do, as most of your income must be given to banks and financial institutions. This is not investing, this is spending!!!!!!

Owning a home within your means, now that MAKES sense! Most financial pundits and institutions say that the purchase price of your home should be roughly 3.5 times your income. (Thus, if you make, say, $100,000 a year, you should buy a house that costs no more than $350,000.) Remember, though, that these financial institutions want you TRAPPED by your home so that you have to get a loan for anything else you need to buy. Profit speaks louder than we do. If you want to be free I recommend that you look at a home to purchase in the range of roughly 1.5 to 2.5 times your income at the MOST.

Intertwined

All three of the hands in your pocket are connected. All the money being created and put into the system causes inflation. (Although the government loves to tell you there isn't any, but all you need to do is compare your household bills for the last five years!) Inflation makes each already imaginary dollar worth less, and punishes anyone saving these dollars, forcing them to spend it and the beat goes on. Debt also causes more taxes (more money in circulation more taxes) and more inflation. Think about that before you charge something or take out that loan.

Why are you telling me all this, Doug? The point is to give you a wake up call! What the future holds for you will depend on your actions today, tomorrow, etc. I am here to tell you right now that it will be a drastically different future if you don't make some changes. You cannot keep the blinders on hoping someone else will fix the economy. You MUST take charge of your own if you want to THRIVE and not simply survive the rest of your days.

Honesty is the Best Policy

A recent survey discovered that 90 percent of Americans either lied about their debt or were in denial about it. Debt will kill your financial freedom; you must get really honest about it. The truth will set you free, but first it will really piss you off, which is good—irritation is often the first step to any long-term significant change. You must make debt your enemy. This mindset along with your new understanding to no longer go along with the "conventional thinking" will lead you out of your debtor prison.

Final Thoughts

How do you escape the prison of debt, inflation and runaway taxes? LIVE BELOW YOUR MEANS. Forget about keeping up with the Jones; they are up to their eyeballs in debt, too. This is going to take work and discipline, and it starts with continuing to read this book. It means continuing to re-educate yourself about money, taxes, inflation, debt and budgeting. It involves creating other income streams besides your job or current business. It begins with changing years (even decades) of bullshit programming, habits and ways of thinking. If you're willing and ready, keep reading and get ready to go to work; if not, set this book on a shelf and later, when the pain gets to be intense enough to do something, pick it back up and get started.

PART 3

The Solution

CHAPTER 7

The Scoreboard and Playbook

I hope by now you realize on a deep, meaningful level how so much of our financial systems and education has been, to put it bluntly, a farce in terms of helping the average American taxpayer. Fear and greed rule, not your well-being. I can continue to share with you stats and charts and numbers showing how the current financial system does not work for YOU, but all you really need to do is look at your bank balance and portfolio. I don't want to come off as Johnny rain cloud. I just want people to understand how things really work—the real rules to the game—so that you can make the best decisions. Once you understand the systems, you can then utilize these to best serve you and address the things that stand in the way of your financial freedom.

To overcome the built-in obstacles and achieve financial freedom requires that you no longer give your money away blindly. You must start managing your own money. To do this you will need a great deal of ongoing education, support, and to read the remainder of this book. Are you ready to move on, break free of the chains of your financial prison? Good, let's go!

Be In It to Win It!

Growing up, I played and loved sports. I hope that you like sports, too. Why? Because you are playing a game right now! You are in the money game (whether you realize it or not). In the money game, the scoreboard is simple: If you are winning, you are financially free. Remember, this is not about how much money you make. I know a lot of people who make a lot of money, yet are completely in financial prison; many of these people are simply broke at a higher level. This is about creating the freedom to do what you want, when you want, without the worry of funding it. You're losing the game if you HAVE TO trade your time and energy away to support your lifestyle; meaning you are living in the financial prison of living paycheck to paycheck.

From a mathematical perspective, how do you know when you have "won" the money game? Simple;

When your ongoing income surpasses your expenses, **you have won!**

Before we go any further... let's address the subject of "Ongoing Income."

It has several names: recurring cash flow, recurrent income, portfolio income and the controversial 'PASSIVE' Income term.

For the purposes of this book, we will call this "Ongoing Income." The reason being the word 'passive' seems to infuse the misconception that one does not have to work for this income. (This is typically associated with scams) However it is my belief that no matter WHAT you call it, if it is income you WORKED (usually hard) to BUILD up for a time (however long) and it now continues to pay you in an ongoing manner consistently over years and years...and it is LEGAL, I would consider it any and all of the above types of Income! It's the BEST kind to have and the only kind that will set you free from the prison of a J-O-B! Now back to our regular programming...

So if you're in it, let's win it. If you are ever going to be free, there is one thing you must do, and that is learn to manage your money. You cannot win the game if you don't know the score.

Here is an added bonus to becoming better at knowing your score and managing your money, you become better at managing your life... and your relationships... and the time you spend with friends... and so on. In other words, you become a happier more fulfilled person.

The Playbook

Every great sports team has a *playbook*, a list of offensive and defensive strategies that help them win the game. The best teams on the planet, the teams who win championships, are the ones who mastered the basics. In football, the basics are blocking, tackling, passing and running the ball. In money, there are some very important defensive strategies that must be in place. I mention three earlier in the book...

1. Hedging against Inflation

2. Reducing your tax Exposure (more to come on that later)

3. Eliminating your debt.

Eliminating debt actually falls into a broader category in the defensive playbook and that is managing your money. The habits you currently have are putting you into debt are the 'plays in your playbook' that are causing you to lose the game and get into debt. Let's explore this further.

Debt Reduction—A MUST

As I mentioned earlier, debt is the No. 1 enemy to financial freedom. I know you have heard a lot of ads about reducing your debt. You hear things like, consolidate your debt, cut your payments in half, and eliminate collection calls. Debt has become a big business. Why? Because there is a ton of money in it. These companies charge you fees and a lot of time get kickbacks from the creditors (predators). I can't see the value of paying another middle man to resolve debt, and it sure in the hell doesn't make sense to take out more debt to pay debt (debt transfer). Now, some may argue about a lower interest rate and blah, blah, blah. They miss the principle—it's *behavior* that gets most people into debt, and if you don't change your behavior, no matter how great the debt consolidation loan is you will end up back in debt (and a lot of times, more in debt than when you began). What happens is this: a person takes out a consolidation loan to pay off the credit cards, and low and behold, they run the cards back up and now they are in twice as deep. *The behavior must change to permanently get rid of debt.* We must get aggressive; we must declare war on the debt-causing habits.

Now the reason most Americans take on debt is because they don't have the funds to purchase something they really want at that moment, so they finance it. As I said earlier, debt is when you spend your future for immediate gratification. To get a handle on debt creating, first we must figure out what you can and cannot afford based on a BUDGET. OOOHH, he said **budget**. Yes, I did. Your budget is your scoreboard to financial freedom. If you are not willing to make and follow a budget, go ahead and close this book and put it on the shelf and just resolve to the fact that things are not going to change for you financially, and you can spend the rest of your life being a victim of your situation. Budgets are that important! They are the scoreboard of your financial life. They will tell you if you're winning or losing the game!!!!

Good, you're still here, let's roll!

In this and the next chapters, I will be laying out some assignments. These are crucial to your financial future. So is your honesty. This first assignment is on budgeting. When most people sit down and do the budget, they bullshit themselves—they really don't know where all the money went, and it's human nature to slant things so they look better than they are. With that said, here is the first assignment to your financial freedom. Complete honesty will be vitally important.

Scoreboard Assignment 1:

Purchase a pocket-sized notebook and pen. Then for the **next 30 days**, write down everything you spend money on for personal reasons (keep business out of it; I hope that you already have a business budget if you're in business). Record EVERYTHING: the latte, a new pair of socks, lunch at McDonalds, everything whether you use cash, check, credit card, or debit card. When you pay a bill, write it in your notebook, too. Then every few days, transfer this info to the daily tracking sheet shown on the following page. For each item, answer whether it is food or shelter with a yes or no only. Then decide what category the expense falls into: food, shelter, entertainment, gifts, debt, etc. (To download this tracking form for free, go to catchfirebook.com.)

In our digital age, we've become desensitized to the value of money. Money has been reduced to figures on an ATM or a computer screen, or a balance on a credit card statement. We've lost touch with what things cost and what we really spend. By recognizing the psychological power of currency and actually tracking and making it real, we discover what we spend.

30 Day Daily Spending Tracking Sheet

Date	Item	Cost	Food or Shelter	Category
TOTAL				

Total non Food and Shelter Items	
Total for Necessary Food and Shelter Items	

Next, look at the categories to see where your money is going. EVERYTHING that is not food and shelter is on the chopping block. EVERYTHING. STEP ONE is to create a bare-bones budget. If you're serious about getting out of debt, here is where it starts. Debt is created when you spent more than you made, so we first must spend less to stop the bleeding. This is going to take sacrifice and the willingness to give up some things. So list out all the things you spent money on in the last month and put a W or a N next to it, because it's either a want or a need.

Example

Groceries $732.16

Haircut $62.49

Rent $1,150.00

Utilities $110.23

Gas $85.00

Cell Phone $99.00

Cable $79.00

Internet $49.00 (separate even if it's a bundled package)

Now let's look at this list. Take groceries, for example. Yes, it's a need, but $732.16 may be way too much. Take a look at what you bought. The potato chips and soft drinks were not needs, they are wants, so reducing your grocery list to only needs should drop the total a couple hundred bucks. Put a N.R. next to it, as it's a need that can be reduced.

O.K., next, haircut. Hmmm, $62.49? Really!!! Yes, a haircut is a need, but this is probably a cut, color, and blow dry done in a salon with a name that most couldn't pronounce. This is something that can be reduced, so put a N.R. next to it.

Now let's take a look at some of the W's (wants). A want is anything that is not work, food, or shelter related. I am not going to tell you that you have to do anything, but if you're serious about getting out of debt and creating financial freedom, here is what I suggest: Answer the following question with each want.

What is more important to me and my family _____(a new I pod)_____(fill in the want) or getting out of debt and being financially free.

Do the same with the needs that can be reduced; answer this question:

What is more important to me excess spending on ___(soda and chips)_____(fill in NR) or my financial freedom.

Please realize that there are no right or wrong answers to these questions, just consequences.

Scoreboard Assignment 2:

Now you should have an honest idea how much is actually going out each month. The next assignment is to figure out exactly what is coming IN and what is going OUT, so you can create a surplus that will help you build your Financial Freedom.

Many feel budgeting is restrictive. Regardless of that, fill this out honestly. This sheet is also downloadable on www.CatchFireBook.com

MONTHLY BUDGETING

INCOME –write down each person in your home that brings home a paycheck and what that is each month. If it is variable income, use an average.

Name:	Average Monthly Income		
Job#1			
Job#2			
Name:			
Job#1			
Job#2			
Other source of Income:			
Other source of Income:			
TOTAL MONTHLY INCOME:			

EXPENSES

Enter in the appropriate amounts in the rows that apply to you.

AUTO	Currently spending Monthly	New budgeted amount	Acct.
Car 1 payment			
Car2 payment			
Car 3 payment			
Average Fuel Bill for cars			
Insurance payments for cars			
Average maintenance bill for cars			
Public Transit/Tolls			
Other:			
HOME	Currently spending Monthly	New budgeted amount	Acct.
Mortgage/Rent			
Average Gas Bill			
Average Electric Bill			
City Services Bill			
Home Insurance			
Property Taxes			
TV bill			
Internet bill			
Home Phone bill			

Average maintenance bill for home			
Other			
HEALTH CARE	Currently spending Monthly	New budgeted amount	Acct.
Health Insurance bill			
Personal care items			
Gym/Fitness membership			
Prescriptions			
Other			
CLOTHING	Currently spending Monthly	New budgeted amount	Acct.
Personal			
Children			
Gear for Sports			
FAMILY/CHILDREN	Currently spending Monthly	New budgeted amount	Acct.
Daycare and babysitting			
Activities, Sports or lessons			
Allowance or child support			
FOOD	Currently spending Monthly	New budgeted amount	Acct.
Grocery bill			
Supplementation			
CELL PHONE	Currently spending Monthly	New budgeted amount	Acct.
Average monthly bill			
ENTERTAINMENT	Currently spending Monthly	New budgeted amount	Acct.
Eating out			
Movies			
Recreation			
Music, Books, Dvd's Playstation, Wii etc..			
Other			

CREDIT CARD/DEBT PAYMENTS	Currently spending Monthly	New budgeted amount	Acct.
Card:			
Card:			
Card:			
Student loans			
Line of credit			
CHARITY/TITHING	Currently spending Monthly	New budgeted amount	Acct.
Tithing or charity			
PETS	Currently spending Monthly	New budgeted amount	Acct.
Food & toys			
Veterinary/Insurance			
MISCELLANEOUS	Currently spending Monthly	New budgeted amount	Acct.
Coffee bar			
Haircuts			
Massage Therapy or Chiropractic			
Life Insurance			
Savings/Investments			
Other			
Other			
Other			
Other			
YEARLY BULK EXPENSES TO AVERAGE OUT	Currently spending Monthly	New budgeted amount	Acct.
AMA membership			
Taxes			
Vacation			
Christmas			
Education/School/Supplies			
Other			
Other			
Other			

Now subtract your monthly expenses from your monthly income....

TOTAL MONTHLY INCOME _____
TOTAL MONTHLY EXPENSES _____
Total SURPLUS or DEFICIT _____

This should be VERY telling as to why you are at where you are at financially.

Many of you will NOT have a SURPLUS; you will have a deficit, which means you are spending more than what is coming in. It is time to CUT back and actually LIVE the lifestyle that is congruent to your income. This may be humbling and require you to put your ego aside. The target is to CREATE a surplus. You will be doing something VERY important with the SURPLUS which you will learn about shortly!

Giving Up Now to Get Ahead and Have it ALL Later!

Now I know I will get some blowback from what I'm about to say, but if you're one of the tens of thousands of students I have worked with, you already know I don't care about things like that. You have to look at this hard; these excess expenses are causing a lot of problems in your life. It's time to get tough. Let's look at some common things that most people are NOT willing to give up and as a result will be in financial prison forever.

1. **Cell Phone:** Listen, I have a mobile phone, but I have it for business and I don't need the one the opens my garage door and has an application that can operate the Mars rover. If our parents and grandparents managed to get by without one, so can we. I have people come up to me

holding a $500 phone telling me how broke and in debt they are. If you are up to your neck in debt, get rid of it!!!!!!

2. **Mortgage:** You have to live somewhere. I get that, but is where you are living within your means? Conventional thinking says that if your house payments are 3.5 times or less of your annual income, you can afford it. So say your annual income is $100,000, and then you could buy a $350,000 house. That is STUPIDLY high if you want to be free. I suggest one to two times your annual income. But Doug, you say, I can't find a house that cheap. Then frickin' rent until you make more money! This is about freedom, and when most people have a hard time making ends meet and slip into debt, it's because they have way too much house for their income. Some of you just went oh, s*#t . Take a deep breath; we have been marketed to and sold the idea that our worth is attached to how our house looks. This all is conventional thinking, which will keep you in debt and that's exactly what the systems want us to be. So it's I owe, I owe, it's off to work I go. So if you're sinking in debt trying to make ends meet, look at your house; if it's more than two times your income, get rid of it even if you lose money on it, because keeping it will cost you your freedom.

3. **Personal Car:** Oh, boy—again, this is one of those areas where pride and ego gets folks good. Keep in mind; *pride and ego are the two most expensive things you can own.* The best car payment is $0, but if that's not possible, a good rule of thumb would be 1/10th of your annual income. In other words, if you make $100,000 a year, a $10,000 car would be about right. Some of you just said, "NO

WAY!" Most folks will buy as much car as the finance company will let them just so they can look good. Again, what's more important, the $40,000 car that's really cool for about a month, or your financial freedom, which is even cooler and lasts forever?

Now I want to talk about the most costly expense for most people. It's so sneaky that the true cost is seldom realized.

4. **The cable or satellite bill:** I know it's only running $60 to $100 a month, but that's not nearly the true cost for most. This costs you your freedom, and it does it in several ways. First it costs you your precious time; most people are in serious denial about how much TV they watch.

According to the A.C. Nielsen Co., the average American watches more than four hours of TV each day (or 28 hours/week, or two months of nonstop TV-watching per year). In a 65-year life, that person will have spent nine years glued to the tube. That's nine years of your life wasted. Do you know how much you could get done in nine years? You can create financial freedom in less than five years.

While losing nine years of your life is bad enough, there are many more costs. Piping in television to your home is like letting the fox in to the hen house. The average child will see 20,000 commercials a year, while the average American will see 2,000,000 commercials in their lifetime. That's right, two *million* sales pitches over a lifetime. Do you think advertisers would spend that kind of money if it didn't work?

When you watch television, every fifteen minutes you are blasted with five to 10 sales pitches. We learn how to spend our money to look cool or be attractive, we learn what to eat and of course who we should trust with our money. Would you allow a door-to-door salesman into your house every 15 minutes? Of course you wouldn't. But as long as those ads come through that box, it's O.K. I get a kick out of folks who have those "NO SOLICITING" signs on their front door, and also have a 50-inch television blasting commercials in the living room.

Also, consider all the violence. The average child will see 200,000 acts of violence before they reach the age of 18. I'm not going to preach here, but that has to have an affect.

Your health also suffers. I can't think of too many things that require less energy and less brain power. As you sit there with your mind mush, they shove information into your brain so we do what they say. Come on, they call it television PROGRAMMING for a reason! Worst of all, the number one advertisers are junk food and fast food, drugs and financial "services" are not far behind. And we wonder why most Americans are overweight and unhealthy, and broke! But that's O.K.; just keep watching and they will sell you a pill to fix it. Television is an expense that, when you add up the costs, just doesn't make sense. *But Doug, I must watch XYZ show; I can't miss it.* O.K., watch it and stay broke and in debt; it has no effect on my life, just yours. My wife always says, "Stop watching other people's lives and start living your own!" Look, I am not hoping to make friends with this book; I am looking to make a difference!

Remember, this is about simplifying your life NOW so you can have it all later. It is the **ultimate** defensive strategy. It is a short term sacrifice for your long term good. People who are broke and in debt are short term thinkers, period. If you do not adopt the habit of thinking long term, you will never be free. Making that transition will be uncomfortable, but will change your life. This is about learning and implementing the basics so you can win the game. Solid money management habits like living within your means will be crucial to the reality of your dreams.

Paying Down the Debt with Your New-found Surplus!

Cutting down your cell phone, TV, mortgage and car bills are a few examples of where you can cut your budget to get to the point where you have a surplus. You can spend a bunch of time clipping coupons, but cutting the pig where it is fattest will make the BIGGEST difference! This is the first step in getting out of debt. Once you have made some cuts, the next step is to use the surplus to pay down the debt.

Let's Get Honest

You must take a hard look at how in debt you are. Review credit card and unsecured debt to see if becoming debt-free in this lifetime is possible. Now I'm not going to suggest you file bankruptcy, but if you have $50-$60,000 of debt, and your income is $40,000, bankruptcy might make sense. My best advice is if you're going to do this, do it right away. Then apply the concepts in this book so you don't end up right back in debt. (The mistake most make is they trying paying down the enormous debt for years and then file bankruptcy, which is a huge waste of money.)

If you really want to pay off your debt, let's get started. First realize that you got into debt systematically; you had a *system* of spending more than you made over a period of time. In order to get out of debt, you will need to do it systematically and over a period of time. It starts with cutting the budget and creating a budget surplus *(which, if you did the assignments earlier in this chapter, you would have done already!).* Then you take the surplus and put it toward your debt above and beyond the regular payment you make.

I suggest one of two systems. You might begin with your smallest debt first, pay extra on it until it's paid off, then take the regular payment you used to make to this debt plus the extra and put it towards the next largest debt. Over time, this begins to snowball. For example, say you have $200 in surplus and your lowest debt is $1,000. Each month you should make your regular payment of $100 plus the $200 surplus until this debt is paid off. Then move to your next debt of, say, $2,000. Make your regular payment (say it's $150) plus the $100 plus the $200 surplus. This will snowball and, over time, kill your debt.

The second method suggests the same system as previously except that you start with the debt with the highest interest rate. When that debt is paid off, you move to the debt with the next highest rate and tackle that.

We have created a software tool to help you with this; it's called the "**DEBT-INATOR**". It's available through our Catch Fire University curriculum.

Once you have paid off your debt, you get to do something WAY more FUN with that surplus. NO, it's *not* going out and buying a bunch of new things!! You will be GROWING your money exponentially with it! Keep reading!

Mastering Money Management

We just talked a lot about budgeting and reducing your debt. That takes money management. Now let's expand that scope so that you manage ALL of your money. There are many money management systems out there, many of them are good. The reason I say that is because the biggest problem with managing money is not a lack of money, but rather lack of a system. You must develop a system that will track your progress and keep score.

Over the years I have read about and seen MANY ways of managing your money, but the best money management system I have ever seen (and the one I use) I learned from T. Harv Eker, my colleague, mentor, and good friend. He is the author of the New York Times number one best selling book *Secrets of The Millionaire Mind* (a must read). I will give you a brief overview of Harv's key concepts, but if you have not yet read the book, STOP, go online, and order it right now while I wait.

O.K., glad you're back. Like most great systems, the concept is simple and brilliant. You start off by dividing your income into different accounts to cover different things. Here are the different accounts:

1. **FFA** (financial freedom account). **10% of your income.** This goes towards investing in things like real estate, ongoing income business, (which we will cover a bit later) and other wealth building strategies.

Note: This is where you begin to play some serious OFFENSE! In an earlier section you created a surplus in your budget; once you have paid off all your debt, that surplus will go entirely to THIS account (over and above the 10%) to EXPEDITE your journey to Freedom! *(Do NOT spend it again on instant gratification; you will end up where you were at!)*

2. **LTSS** (long term savings for spending). **10% of your income.** Use this account to save up to buy higher-ticket items, such as a new car, flat screen TV, new computer, great vacation, college fund, Christmas etc.

3. **EDUCATION. 10% of your income.** This should be used for your ongoing education, books, seminars etc.

4. **PLAY. 10% of your income.** Yes, an account for you to have guilt-free fun. Shopping sprees, trip to the spa, new golf clubs, tickets to a sports game, a night of fine dining or whatever makes you feel amazing and free.

5. **GIVE. A minimum of 5% of your income.** Use this account for charity and worthy causes you would like to support.

6. **NECESSITY. 55% of your income.** This money goes toward paying the bills: your rent, your mortgage, lights, groceries, etc.

So it's simple: open up six accounts at your bank, and then as you get paid, divide up and place your after-tax dollars into the appropriate accounts. (If your income isn't taxed, then you need another account, a TAX account.) The percentages are flexible; I think the ones suggested are a great target. This system is powerful if you use it and as I said, it is the system my wife and I personally use. For more information about this system and about a million other helpful things, read *Secrets of the Millionaire Mind* or go to the seminar The Million Mind Intensive (schedule is available at peakpotentials.com).

Scoreboard Assignment# 3

Take your MONTHLY budgeting sheet and mark WHICH expenses FALL into WHICH Accounts. There is ALREADY a space for you to fill this out on the chart. It is the column with "Acct"; simply put an N for Necessity, P for Play, E for Education and so on.

Once you have completed this, see where you are compared to the recommended percentages. You may need to be flexible on some item or on some percentages, but no matter what, know this: THIS entire process of cutting, budgeting, paying off debt and managing your money alone could set you free. It may take awhile, but that is irrelevant. Later on in the book I will talk about increasing you income to accelerate your journey to Financial Freedom.

A Final Note

In this last chapter we covered the Scoreboard to your Financial Life and the most important defense strategy: great money management skills! These are a must in order to become financially free. I know that some of you reading this are thinking, *I hate money management, it's so analytical and tedious.* I understand. But it's a lot better than a life of struggle and ending up working until your last breath. Even if you make a LOT of money, if you do not manage it well, you will never be free. Now let's talk about Offense.

CHAPTER 8

Mind Your Own Business

Here are the cold, hard facts: 95 percent of Americans are not financially free. A big reason why this happens is that we have been programmed to believe in what I call the 67-Year Plan. Around the age of five, you go off to school. Why? So you can learn both information and how to follow directions so that when you graduate, you can… get a good job. You then spend the 67 years of your life (give or take) working and, we hope, saving for retirement. Then along about age 72, you "retire" and move south, where you buy white shoes and play shuffle board three times a week with other retirees. You then proceed to live out your Golden Years on the retirement savings you built up over your working career.

There are two problems with this programmed plan: one, it takes 67 years (of your best years, too), and two, it doesn't work! As countless studies and statistics show us, the vast majority of Americans simply can't save enough to retire to a life of ease.

Having said all that, let's look at the five percent who do become financially free. How did they achieve this financial freedom? In almost every case, *the financially free among us achieved their freedom through business.* In other words, they became a business owner, and then built and sustained a successful business. I have never—repeat, never—met someone who achieved financial freedom through working for someone else.

Building a business is the Offense strategy in the Playbook. It will increase your income and accelerate your journey to freedom. Remember, your budgeting surplus, which is now going into your FFA account, can help to "fund" your new business endeavor. Just managing your money can set you free, but it will take much longer. Most are not that patient. I know I'm not.

Here's the shortcut: You need to build a particular *kind* of business.

Let me explain.

As I've mentioned, early in my life I built and owned a series of traditional businesses. Over time these became profitable and successful. In fact, to be honest, I made quite a bit of money during this time. But a funny thing happened on the way to the bank, as they say: As my business grew, so did its complexity. I had to spend more and more time on "little" things like human resources, budgeting, and so on. It got to the point where even though I was "the boss", I felt like I was in a financial prison. Yes, I had my own business. But business ownership wasn't giving me the two things I really wanted—more time and more money.

Business is supposed to set you *free*! If you still have to go to an office or a place of business and perform your services or run the business, you are not free. Basically, what you have done is trade a job at an employer for a business where you have hired yourself to be the sole employee. Again, this is NOT freedom ringing!

What the ultra-successful five percent of the people have developed—and which I then realized and developed—is a business *where you make money regardless of whether you work or not in the business.* This is called ongoing income. Again, you still must build a business. But you build a business that, ultimately, runs on its own, without your day-to-day involvement. In other words, someone has to work, it just isn't you!

To create an ongoing income business requires systemization. One you get the business established and off and running, it should run (virtually) by itself. Now some of you might find this, well, off-putting. You *want* to be the boss, the "man"; you *want* that adrenaline rush of landing the big new client, or drawing off your home equity loan to fund next week's employee payroll. No! To create an ongoing income business, *you must take your ego out of the equation.* Financially free people don't really care about being the "star CEO" of a business. They want the automatic systemization, the recurring revenue, and the resulting more time and more money.

Here's something else to realize about an ongoing income business: We have been programmed literally since birth to work the "traditional" way, i.e., exchange hours for dollars. Creating an ongoing income business simply isn't on the radar screen of the vast majority of people. And for those who are aware of it, most people believe it's too complex or too fraught with potential pain to accomplish. Not the case!

FLASH POINT

Creating passive income is no harder than obtaining regular income, it's just different.

Business Criteria: Dougonomics: 5 Crucial Criteria When Looking for a SUCCESSFUL Business.

I believe these five criteria are necessary not only for building a successful business, but building one that creates true financial freedom. Please note: If you choose a business and ALL criteria are not met, I cannot make any promises that your endeavor will provide a long-term solution to freedom and wealth. I do know from personal experience that if these five elements are met, it will ensure a successful business that will pay you... even if you are in a coma!

Business Criteria 1: Be in Business FOR Yourself But Not BY Yourself

I believe that, regarding their careers and finances, people can be generally classified one of three ways:

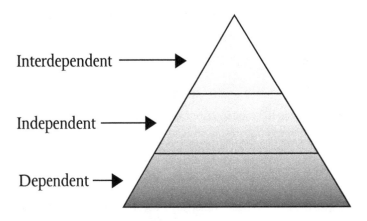

Let's explore each of these segments.

Who is DEPENDENT?

Employee's, Disability, Welfare

As an **employee**, you are **DEPENDENT!** In other words, your income is dependent on someone else (your employer). You have no control over your own well being. If it makes financial sense for the company you work for to get rid of you, they WILL! It doesn't matter how long or hard you have worked for the company. It doesn't matter how much your boss loves you. The bottom line is, when you gotta go, you'll be gone.

It's not only more difficult to become financially free as an employee, it's darn near impossible!

Who is INDEPENDENT?

Small business owners, and private practice professionals like lawyers, doctors, chiropractors, consultants, etc.

INDEPENDENT people are those who are typically self-employed. It's all up to you! You do all the work, or you are busy babysitting adults to ensure they do the work.

Yes, independent folks are not held victim to one client (you have many). But very few of these folks have true leverage. Why? *You only get paid when you perform the work.* Once you stop working, then you are screwed! Once you stop working, the money stops, too. The self-employed retirement statistics would scare Godzilla. They are worse than those who are employed.

Who is INTERDEPENDENT?

Businesses, companies and entrepreneurs who co-create (with someone else) win-win partnerships, like Google, Donald Trump, etc.

Being **INTERDEPENDENT** is the key to creating a successful business. It is all about developing win-win partnerships. True leverage happens when both parties have equal to gain. Please note, this is rare, but once it happens, it is hugely powerful.

Donald Trump is a great example of an Interdependent Business man. He creates win-win partnerships in his various business ventures.

When evaluating or building a business, it must be Interdependent. You want to find key alliances and partnerships where both parties can leverage off of the other. This comes down to finding and building key relationships in the right networks. I've never met a happy, wealthy hermit.

Business Criteria 2: The Business Must Ultimately Provide Ongoing and Unlimited Income

Why is this important? HELLO! Why wouldn't you want to be in a business that would provide an opportunity for UNLIMITED income potential? Remember, a job can never provide this. Or let me put it this way: if you are going to put your *efforts in*, you want the *most* out of those efforts, yes? Successful people are always looking for the best return on their investments no matter if it is time or money they are investing!

As we mentioned before, ongoing income has several names, but the concept remains the same. **Nonetheless here is the indisputable fact: without ongoing income, you can never truly be financially free!**

FLASH POINT

Ongoing Income is when I get paid on a profitable action(s) without having to be there for it.

Here's an example. My wife and I recently bought a property in Texas for cash. We hired a management company to rent the place out and they take care of everything for us. Because we paid cash for it, we have no mortgage and it cash-flows 100%. Each month we get paid with no work on our part.

We also have an Internet and affiliate marketing company which generates hundreds of thousands of dollars a year for us... even if we are out of the country on vacation.

NOTE: all ongoing income businesses take work to start and build, and only a little to maintain. Be very wary of anyone that tries to sell you a 'get rich quick' scheme.

Again, ongoing income is not running a large, traditional business. I know *so* many multi-millionaire business owners who are a slave to their business or venture.

Ask yourself this question: "Does what I am doing currently have the capacity to create an ongoing income, or am I simply trading hours for dollars?"

Next, ask yourself this question: "Does what I am doing currently have *unlimited* income potential, or is there a *cap* on what I can make?"

If freedom is what you desire, you must start looking for an unlimited ongoing income potential in your next endeavor.

Business Criteria 3: Develop a Multi-Industry (not Single Industry) Opportunity

Are you familiar with Wal-Mart? COSTCO? What about Target? These companies are PRIME examples of multi–industry businesses. Multi-industry businesses are great if:

- you want your business to be good in good times and *great* in bad times.

- you want to move *with* the market and market trends, to help you always stay profitable.

- you want to be profitable no matter *what* the economy does.

The *flexibility* that comes with a multi-industry business is *crucial* to the long-term life span and profitability of a business. To put this point another way, you do not want to be product specific or industry dependent.

Single Industry

If you rely on the sale of any one product or service, you will be a slave to the swings in market trends. For example, if you are in the travel industry, the mortgage industry, the juice industry, or the massage therapy industry, you are a *single* industry business that will be (at one time or another) a victim to the external circumstances of the economy. You will do "good in good times" but you'll also do *terrible* in bad times.

Being in a single industry business also means you will have to constantly engage and land new customers for your product and service to replace the ones you lost. This creates a vicious cycle that will never set you free.

Multi-Industry

Wal-Mart, COSTCO, and Target are great examples of a multi-industry business model. They carry EVERYTHING, and everything they carry is in a multitude of different industries. Automotive, house wares, clothing, electronics, grocery, eye care, the list goes on and on. In doing this they have created what's called a *share of customer*. Let me explain. Instead of constantly marketing for new customers it goes something like this...When you go into COSTCO with your list of items, do you usually come out with exactly what was on your list, or more than what was on your list? Yes, exactly...MORE! In business, this means *fewer* customers can create *more sales* (volume) than a single industry business.

Riding the Waves: *creating a multi-industry business is also a must if you want to be in a position where you can change with the times.* This way, you can ride the market, trend and economy waves rather than be swamped down by them, setting yourself free in the process.

Business Criteria 4: Create an Information Age (Not Industrial Age) Business Model

I do not want to do business in an Industrial Age business model! Why? *Because we live in the Information Age!* I want my business to be able to change with the times! Let me explain.

INDUSTRIAL AGE MODEL:

During the Industrial Age, a business or person developed an idea for a product, then probably produced a few prototypes, maybe got some investors together and secured funding, etc. Then they created a manufacturer to make the product, distributors to distribute it, and retailers to carry and sell it. Then they needed to invest tens of thousands or even millions to market this product to the masses to convince them that they needed this product.

INFORMATION AGE:

Today, we don't create products first, and try to sell them later. Now, we attempt to discover what people want, then build those products. We survey, collect information, analyze it to find out what the consumer wants, *then* we go out and get this product and provide it to them. Marketing and selling becomes a breeze. Why? *They already said they wanted it!* All you are doing is bringing it to them! This is often done electronically (though sometimes manually).

Starbucks is a great example of this. Although a single industry business (coffee, and its variations and accompaniments), Starbucks asks for your information *before* they create your drink. They have become famous for coffee drinks *any way you want it.* Starbucks, in other words, it the *only* place my wife can go and ask for her *Grande* iced soy decaf half-sweet Caramel Macchiato, easy on the caramel and served upside down…and they don't look at her weird! This, folks, creates a life-long customer!

Many Internet businesses today are prime examples of the Information Age model. However, most are just Billboards on the Internet; don't confuse the two, it can be a costly mistake. If they are truly information-based, they are a collection point of useful information to accommodate the consumer now and in the future.

What's more, an Information Age business will usually have lower overhead costs and be more efficient, and therefore be more profitable. And Information Age businesses on the Internet will have a *far* greater chance of generating ongoing income than any other.

Not to beat this point, but the danger of being an Industrial Age business is that they are often tied to being product or industry specific. Take Smith Corona. Do you know that at one point, they were the one of *largest* companies in North America? They manufactured typewriters. But then a little something called the word processor came along. Smith Corona did *not* move with the times. Why? Because shifting an industrial model business can be an extremely large and expensive project. Because Smith Corona did not take the risk to change their core products, they went out of business!

The United States is no longer in the Industrial Age. It's OVER. We are no longer the manufacturing moguls we once were. We are now in our information age! If you want to do an Industrial Age business, move to China or India, they are in their Industrial Age!

Business Criteria 5: Develop or use a Proven Business System

When I was younger, someone very wise once told me this: "You only need one good idea to make it big." So I spent the next eight years coming up with great ideas and trying to make them work. But then I realized the second half of that statement: *the good idea didn't have to be* my *idea!* WOW! After that revelation, I was financially free in just a few short years!

> ## FLASH POINT
>
> It is so *much* simpler to model success than
> to re-invent the wheel!

Go find business models that are working, select one that meets the other four criteria, and then dive in!

Now, I don't want to discourage entrepreneurs and others who have new business ideas. If you want to develop something new, go for it. My advice is not to put all your eggs in one basket or have your entire financial life dependent on its success. I have people come up to me all the time with ideas for a business and they ask me if I think it will work. The best answer I can give is this: "I DON'T KNOW!" I don't know if it will work or not. I'm much more comfortable pointing to successful business models and systems, and saying this: "I *know* that this has been proven to work."

I suggest that you get financially free *first*, then you can try all the ideas, dreams and concepts you have and no matter whether they work or not, you can still eat!!

These five criteria are crucial to creating a long lasting, very profitable business that will set you free. Being financially bullet-proof is one of the most powerful things you can do for both YOUR economy and THE economy!

And one more point before we move on: Can you have more than one ongoing income business? Yes! Just don't get greedy or over-extend yourself by working on two or three at the same time. Get one done first, than move on to others.

The "W" Word—Work

As you can see, developing a successful ongoing income business is going to take some work on your part. You need to do your homework, do some research, poke around a bit. You'll probably have to read some articles, even books, maybe even attend a seminar or two. Be sure that if you are building your own or leveraging your time and money by choosing an already existing ongoing income business that you do your homework, due diligence and that you have support from others who have been successful. The important thing to remember is this: *learning about financial freedom isn't enough; you must also take action!* In other words, it's nice to sit in the lawn chair drinking a fruity drink with a little umbrella sticking out of it. But at some point you gotta jump into the pool. If not NOW…when?

"But Doug, I've got a job. I can't learn this on my own."

"But Doug, I'm not that smart when it comes to numbers."

"But Doug, I'm a busy person. How can I learn how to manage my own money when I'm so busy (my job, with the kids, golfing, playing poker, [insert your excuse])?"

I have to admit, I get tired when people keep showing me their "butts." However, on some level I do "get it": Why don't more people become financially free? They're too busy working! Here is the truth of it: If you don't MAKE time, you will NEVER have time. Period.

Let me tell you something bluntly: You can make money or you can make excuses, but you cannot make both. It's your choice. I suggest you choose financial freedom. It's right here for the taking. And if you don't choose financial freedom, that's O.K. But just do me and all the other people in your life one big favor: Stop bitching about the bills, work, your lack of time and how tired you are and the path you have chosen, which is to be exactly where you're at.

A Final Note

Each of us has that little voice inside our head telling us how busy we are, how many other obligations we have. Here's what you do. Each time that little voice in your head rants and raves and spews forth all the reasons why you can't do something, remember that listening to this little voice your whole life has gotten you into this mess in the first place. Yes, this will take time. Yes, you are busy. But if you want financial freedom bad enough, trust me, you *will* make it happen.

> ### FLASH POINT
>
> *Your financial success will depend on what you do in your spare time.*

CHAPTER 9

Be a TOOL!

We are the tool that creates our life, including our finances. As much as we all want to, individually you are not going to change the current financial and economic systems, get the banks to play fair, stop taxes, or put a halt to inflation. The one thing you can change, however, is *you*, specifically how you deal with the systems. The buck starts and stops with you. Period.

I am a realist. I know the vast majority of people who finish this book will put it on a shelf and life will go back to "business as usual." Those folks simply aren't willing to do the one thing necessary to get different results, and that is to CHANGE. While easy, staying the same also makes life difficult.

We must have a very good reason to go through the uncomfortable process of change. Why? We all have been programmed to take the easy way out. Look at almost every product and service advertised; virtually all are designed to make life easy. Just take this pill and you will lose weight; or, rub on this cream and you will look 10 years younger. And one of my personal favorites: Give us your money and never worry about retirement again. Our whole society has been built on comfort and ease, doing just enough to "get by." The result? The vast majority of Americans just get by. In my opinion, just getting by really, really SUCKS! In this country of opportunity, where people risk their lives *everyday* to live here, getting by is like kissing through a screen door—it sure looks like you're doing something, but you're not. Change isn't easy!! If it were, everybody would be rich and free!!! Let me share with you this—I found that creating financial success in my life was *easier* than being broke and in financial prison with no control over my life.

This is a turning point for you. Decide right flippin' now—are you truly ready to do the work? If so, here are the steps to change:

1. Get Irritated

2. Get Motivated

3. Get Educated

4. Get Activated

GET IRRITATED

While not easy, change is simple. Like I mentioned earlier, first you need a strong, compelling reason to change. When you break it down, there are only two reasons we do things: either the carrot and the stick or pleasure and pain. It has been my experience working with tens of thousands of people that pain or the stick is more powerful. I have also discovered that the pleasure or carrot is far more powerful after you have felt the stick. So to take the first step in changing your situation you must get **IRRITATED.**

FLASH POINT

Every success story starts with someone getting really pissed off.

I am grateful that my point of irritation happened very early, when I was about nine-years-old. I had to go to school wearing a pair of hand-me-down shoes. These weren't just any hand-me-down's, they were my older sister's tennis shoes. Now I may have gotten away with this... except for the pink striping on the shoe's heel. The result? For that entire school year my nick name was 'Doug-a-rina.' I was seriously pissed and made a vow that I would never live in poverty like this. Wearing used clothes and eating government-provided cheese sandwiches was not going to be my life. I didn't know *how* I was going to escape this life, but I knew there was more in store for me.

I had become really irritated. Nothing great ever happens until someone gets seriously irritated. You have to get to the point were enough is enough and you're not going to take it anymore.

While writing this book, I have had a few friends read it. One, a dear friend of mine, told me that he got angry reading the book, and wanted me to add a couple lines in to soften it. I have a lot of respect for him, so I thought about it long and hard. In the end, though, I decided not to soften some of the things I had written. This stuff *should* tick you off!!! Being misinformed and lied to about money your whole life and ending up broke *should* anger and irritate you, hopefully enough for you to do something about it.

The Pacifiers, Distractions and Pills

So why aren't people pissed? Why aren't people rioting in the street? Well, most people don't know how our systems work (or don't work for them). They are lazy and ignorant and it is easier to put their head in the sand and pretend everything is fine. Oh, they will bitch and complain and play the "poor me victim," but to do and learn something new, that's out of the question.

Instead of changing, most folks simply numb the pain. Many people suck on pain pills, pacifiers and hold fast to their distractions to avoid becoming aware of the reality of the situation. They do this with a wide variety of compulsions and addictions, from television to drugs. I know firsthand the train wreck addiction can cause, having had my own battles with it. I am thankful mine was alcohol, something obvious that people saw and then convinced me to get help. Many compulsions aren't so obvious. It's the "comfort activities" that can steal your potential. These activities prevent us from doing new things because they have us stuck in old habits. Here are a few (though by no means all) of these comfort activities:

1. Food

2. Television

3. Video games

4. Pain/Illness *(Yes, some people are addicted to their pain. Who would they be without it? What would they talk about? You ALL know people like this. Pain has become their excuse NOT to move forward in their lives.)*

5. Internet

6. Cleaning

7. Shopping/Spending

8. Being BUSY and having "too much on my plate"

9. Workaholic

10. Drugs and Alcohol

11. Gambling

12. Sex

This obviously is not a complete list, and doesn't include the number one thing people are addicted to: that, of course, is DRAMA. I'll get to that in a moment. If you think you may have a problem with any of these compulsions (or another not mentioned), GET HELP now. I'm serious; put this book down now and go find help! There are support groups and resources available for just about any compulsion. If you have a serious compulsion or addiction, you simply won't feel the true pain of your situation, and real change will be impossible.

Drama Queens/Kings

You have all heard the saying "shit happens." And it does. I am the first to know that DRAMA, however, is OPTIONAL. A flat tire, the flu, a broken arm, getting stuck in traffic, your computer crashes, etc... it is all bound to happen. This is called *LIFE*. However, many get sucked into making a big deal out of it and letting these random events control their life. You all know people like this, there is *always* something going on. Focusing on this part of life sucks the energy out of the more positive productive parts of life. When shit happens and you give it energy, you create drama. It's tiring being around people like this. I would much rather be around people who focus their energy on where they are going and not on what just happened. This is *forward* thinking, not reverse thinking. This type of behavior will make it impossible to create financial freedom in your life. It is vitally important you watch your thoughts and actions throughout the day. Many who would normally NOT categorize themselves as drama kings and queens in fact are, and will spin their wheels until they get honest.

Now it's time to get to work on getting pissed.

EXERCISE 1.1

For this exercise, please commit to complete honesty, and give yourself permission to get emotional, even angry. There is no room for rationalizing and justifying. Every person who has made it to the top has touched the bottom. Answer the following questions by writing out the answers right now. If a question does not apply to you, skip it and go to the next one.

1. How much am I in debt, and how do I feel about being foolish enough to get into debt?

_____

_____

_____

_____

_____

_____

_____

2. What is my current income? (Keep in mind there are people who aren't any smarter than you making billions.) How do I feel about making this amount?

_____

_____

_____

_____

_____

_____

_____

3. Since 95% of North Americans will NEVER retire to the lifestyle they desire AT ALL, how do I feel about the imminent possibility that I will be working until I die, or living in poverty in my golden years?

_____

_____

_____

_____

_____

4. How much have I put away for my children's college? If it's not enough, how do I feel about telling my kids that they may have to take out loans to go to college and start life in debt?

_____

_____

_____

_____

_____

5. How does it feel to work for someone else and to be told where to go, when to be there, and to have to ask permission to take a day off?

_____

_____

_____

_____

_____

6. How does it feel to have most of my dreams die?

_____

_____

_____

_____

_____

_____

7. When I have to miss family functions because of work, I feel:

_____

_____

_____

_____

_____

_____

8. When I receive my bills and/or collection calls, I feel:

_____

_____

_____

_____

_____

_____

EXERCISE 1.2

Next, write a **"I'm mad as hell and I am not going to take it anymore"** statement.

Example:

I'm mad as hell and I'm not going to take it anymore. I will not continue to live paycheck to paycheck, losing sleep each night *wondering how I'm going to make ends meet. I will not continue to live afraid of checking the mail because of the bills and late notices. I have had it with collection calls. I have had it with my family not getting the lifestyle they deserve. I will not miss more family functions because I had to work, etc...*

"I'm mad as hell and I am not going to take it anymore...

The point to all of this is to clear out all the distractions and rationalizations and all the crap we tell ourselves, such as it's O.K. to struggle. Once you have written your statement, read it out loud. Now, allow yourself to feel the anger and irritation. Do NOT allow your mind to justify your current situation or tell you things are fine; as long as you keep telling yourself your situation is "O.K. and everything will be fine", your life will not change. Finally, place your statement on your bathroom mirror at home and read it twice a day.

Some of you might be thinking that this is focusing on the negative. It's not! I want you to remove your rose colored glasses and look objectively at your situation. Being honest and real and getting angry about your life at this moment is good energy that can translate into change.

Now that we have the stick in place, let's move on to the carrot.

GET MOTIVATED

mo·ti·vate (m t-v t) To provide with an incentive; move to action; impel. mo ti·va tor n. motivate.

Next, we must use this energy of irritation as an incentive to become motivated. In order to become motivated and to stay motivated, we need really good "reasons." We as humans never do anything without a good reason.

So the question becomes this: What would financial freedom do for you? Imagine for a minute what being free would be like; not having to go to work, having more time, no worries regarding how to pay the bills, etc. What would your life be like? Who would you BE? What would you be DOING? What would you HAVE? What could you GIVE? Remember, if you can't conceive it, you won't achieve it, so access that child within you that dreams BIG!!

It's time to get crystal clear regarding the reasons for you to become financially free.

EXERCISE 2.0

Now, list all the things **you would do** and all the things you would **personally have** (this one's about you). Come up with at least 25.

1 _____

2 _____

3 _____

4 _____

5 _____

6 _____

7 _____

8 _____

9 _____

10 _____

11 _____

12 _____

13 _____

14 _____

15 _____

16 _____

17 _____

18 _____

19 _____

20 _____

21 _____

22 _____

23 _____

24 _____

25 _____

I know some of you had no problem coming up with 25 things for yourself, while most got stuck on about number three. For most, the dream of being financially free is just that—a dream. Without an actual way and plan to create financial freedom, it becomes painful to even think about. In turn, you stop thinking about it and it never happens.

FLASH POINT

What you think about comes about,
and what you don't think about…doesn't.

If you don't have 25, keep working on this exercise until you do. Keep in mind that these things are for you. When you have 25 for you, move on to the next exercise.

EXERCISE 2.1

Now I want you to list what you would do for others once you are financially free and don't have to spend 40+ hours a week exchanging your life for a paycheck. How would you serve your family, your community, your friends, and the world?

1 _____

2 _____

3 _____

4 _____

5 _____

6 _____

7 _____

8 _____

9 _____

10 _____

11 _____

12 _____

13 _____

14 _____

15 _____

16 _____

17 _____

18 _____

19 _____

20 _____

21 _____

22 _____

23 _____

24 _____

25 _____

Again, keep working on this until you have 25.

EXERCISE 2.2

Now, pick five from each list that are the most powerful and desirable, the things that excite you the most and that you are the most passionate about. Next, set a date for financial freedom. Make it doable, but don't set it out 20 years; three to five years is a reasonable timeline.

What actions will you take on a daily, weekly, and monthly basis to create your financial freedom and to make the five things from your lists a reality?

Understand you may not have ALL the puzzle pieces YET, but you HAVE to start somewhere; if you don't, things will never change. Your target statement is a living entity that grows as you do. So the spots that seem blank and empty in your mind *will* get clear as you move forward.

You may notice that I have chosen to use the term 'Target' instead of goals in this book. Target implies something specific that you first focus on; aim at; then shoot for. If missed you simply aim and shoot again using the knowledge you learned from the shot missed. The term "goals" is thrown around a lot and seems to have lost its meaning. In sports there is always somebody trying to stop you from making a goal, and if you miss, you may not get another chance. Not with target's! You can always do more target practice. There is also no chance of failure so as long as you continue to shoot for your specific target you will inevitably hit it!

NOW, you are going to create your Financial Freedom Target Statement. Write it as if you already did all the work and have achieved it, so it is based in the future but written in the present tense. Here's an example:

Today is (insert your desired date) and I am financially free. This has allowed me to fire my boss and spend more time home with my family. I will take that second honeymoon with my wife by going to Hawaii for two weeks. This extra time also will allow me to write my novel. And so on, and so on....

The more detailed the statement, the better.

My financially free life looks like this:

Today is ...

_____

_____

_____

_____

_____

_____

_____

_____

_____

Put this statement next to your "I'm mad as hell" statement and read it twice a day, too. You need to keep one eye on the prize and the other on the pain at all times. As you hit one target, take another from one of the lists of 25 and add it to the statement.

There is SO much more to creating powerful target statements, much of which does not work in a book format. In fact, this is something so powerful that we go through an entire module on it in our Catch Fire University.

GET EDUCATED

Now let's move on to Education. We are all educated; the question is, what are you educated to do and not to do? For the answer, look at your results.

Our current education system was modeled on systems designed to create soldiers and factory workers. Doesn't it strike you as odd that you can go through 12 to 20 years of education in this country and never learn how money really works, who makes the rules, and how to play the game? It's no wonder so many people struggle.

Our society reaffirms the system by telling us to get a good job and work hard and give your money away to other people so they can invest it for us. They tell us to buy, buy, buy and go into debt, debt, debt.

For most, it's like playing a game where no one informed you on the RULES, HOW to SCORE, how to play Defense, and so on. In other words, it's like playing a game to win… but you don't know how to measure victory! It's no wonder why the masses struggle and the few (who know the game) get really rich.

FLASH POINT

Not only do I consider being broke a social disease,
it has become an epidemic.

Living paycheck to paycheck is a trap most fall into; however, for those who know there is a way out, many choose to stay. Being broke perpetuates itself. Not only do I consider being broke a social disease, it has become an epidemic. This is especially true when those who are broke continue to hang around others who are broke, reinforcing the validity of their situation. These folks NEVER seek an outside perspective; and don't they love to CONDEMN the rich rather than LEARNING from them. This results in the spread of the "epidemic" from person to person, generation to generation. This creates an environment where the disease can grow and spread. Understand that you are the average sum of the people within your network. If your life was a PLAYGROUND and the people or 'playmates' on the playground WITH you are your friends and family and co-workers, you WILL be LIKE them, and you will all VALIDATE the situations you are in. Broke, slave to a job, condemning the rich, whatever you all share. Getting educated, on the other hand, changing and learning another way, would be OUTSIDE the parameters of the playground, and most are far too attached to "being RIGHT" and staying SAFE and "comfortable" to escape the clutches of the disease. I cannot help these people until they are willing to change playgrounds and learn from someone else.

Here's the rub: if you have read this far in this book, you KNOW the "I didn't know" excuse doesn't work anymore. You have learned that the 401(k) is a scam, that education and a good job doesn't equal financial security and that our so-called Social Security will NOT take care of you in your golden years.

You have learned that your DEFENSE playbook MUST include hedging against inflation, eliminating your debt, and reducing your tax exposure.

You will learn later in this book what EXTERNAL strategies should be in your OFFENSIVE playbook. Learning and continuing your education is essential to your success; without ongoing education and learning, you will continue to tread water where you are at. That's a promise.

But first, there are some INTERNAL shifts and skills you must learn to create true and lasting financial freedom. Let me describe a few of these essential skills.

Essential Skill #1 Leadership

Top of the list is **Leadership**. Many believe great leaders are born, not made. I couldn't disagree more. Leadership is a learnable skill. Many of you might believe that you already know how to lead others. Again, in my opinion, if someone thinks that way, they don't know sh#t about leadership. Leaders understand the importance of learning; they are always feeding their mind.

How can you rate your current leadership skills? It's simple—look at your life! The first person you lead is yourself. Look at the quality of your relationships, your financial situation, your health, weight, and fitness. Look at your current job or career. YOU and you alone have LED yourself to exactly where you are RIGHT now! So, how do you rate? If you do not like what you see, you must work on your leadership skills FIRST and FOREMOST with yourself *before* you can begin to lead others. There is an OLD saying I love: "Lead by EXAMPLE." Why do bookshelves and online bookstores contain thousands of books and courses on leadership? Because it's that important!!!! Now I am not going to pretend that I can teach leadership in a book; that would insult your intelligence! But we have dedicated an entire module to it in our Catch Fire University.

Essential Skill #2 Sales

Another must: **Sales** skills. If you're going to create financial freedom in this lifetime, business almost certainly will be involved, and no business lasts long without sales. Again this is something we teach in our university. (Hmmmm, you still haven't checked us out on the web, at **www.catchfirebook.com**? What does that say about your commitment to making positive change?) The truth is we sell every day: our ideas, our opinions, we sell our children on certain behaviors, etc. In my experience, every highly successful person that I've met has been a fantastic salesperson. Many have a negative association with selling due to being harassed by a vacuum cleaner sales man, bothered by an over excited MLM'er or burned by a "deal." The sales skills we will be teaching in the University are about professionalism. I'm referring to the process of professionally presenting your product in a way that people will see its real value. Again there are whole books on the subject and if I were to teach this subject I could not do it in one chapter either.

Essential Skill #3 Marketing

Marketing, the ability to expose your products and services to as broad and yet precise potential market as possible, also is a financial freedom must. If marketing makes you think about the standard mass marketing that they still teach in college, you are in for a big disappointment. There are ways to create millions of dollars in sales without spending a dime. I know this to be true because I have done it.

Social media marketing, in this day and age, has become a must to stay competitive in business. This Internet thing is catching on, and if you are not keeping up to speed you will get pummeled in the market place. There are ways to promote your product or service and touch thousands of people for FREE or at very little cost.

Essential Skill #4 Presentation skills

Presentation skills, the ability to present ideas and products in a way that entertains, educates, and represents its true value, also are a must. I have a lot of experience in this area; I have sold over $100 million of products and services with my presentation skills. Doing presentations in front of several people is a high form of leverage; presenting to thousands of people at the same time increases your volume by thousands. I fully realize that public speaking remains most people's number one fear, but by overcoming this fear it will allow you to grow immensely. Think about this: if you kick your number one fear's ass, how easy would it be to do the same to your second, third, and fourth fears? Pretty darn easy, right? Great presentation skills will spread your value farther, make you rich and can set you free.

Essential Skill #5 Investing skills

Investing Skills will definitely be a must. Most people have learned investing from the system, which is designed to get your money. In doing so, you shoulder all the risk while they keep most of the money and every once in a while, they give you some crumbs. Investing this way leads to a very late retirement, and even possibly spending your retirement in a breezeway handing out shopping carts. The rich (and educated) investors invest in a completely different way; if you learn this way and invest like rich people, guess what—you end up rich, free and enjoying your life. For many the first step is getting out of debt, increasing your income and then you can invest to build your wealth without banking your entire financial life on it. Wherever you are right now you must learn these strategies. In our Catch Fire University, you will have an opportunity to learn from and even do business with the best in business.

Essential Skill #6 Self Mastery

Mastering yourself will be one of the most important skills you can acquire. The only thing that can stop you is you. Ego and false pride, as well as all of the information and misinformation you have learned, are the only things standing in the way of your freedom. Most of the obstacles in your way are self-created fears, beliefs or drama, and unless you are already free, you have not mastered yourself or your finances yet. When you have set your pride and ego aside and you begin to learn how to get out of your own way, the journey begins and it doesn't have to take long. This is a must, and we do some serious work on this in the University.

These are just a few of the skills needed to create the life of freedom and abundance. We cover these and many more in our University. Now please note: our University is not the only place to learn these skills; there are many great teachers out there conducting seminars and workshops on these subjects. These seminars are great, *providing you have the money and the time.* You can easily spend $2,000 to $5,000 in tuition and another $1,000 to $2,000 in travel expense for just one subject. Plus, you must be away from home and work for two or three or five days. You could easily spend $100,000 and a lot of lost work time on your education. I did it, and it is so worth it. But realistically, most people don't have the means or the time. This is why I created the University—so that you can get all the information you need online, working around your schedule, at a fraction of the cost, and with zero airport or hotel time. Whether you use us or someone else, just get the education.

Activation:

Here is where most people fall down: in order to achieve success in anything, you must take action, and to change your life, you need to take MASSIVE and consistent ACTION. Complacency and procrastination stops most people from achieving their dreams. This is where our programming kicks in. If we want something different, we have to do something different. All the 'risk' happens when we take action. Most fear failure, some even fear success; either way, things will change after different actions are taken consistently. The only way to truly fail is to *not take any action*. To put this point another way, we must move beyond our current "comfort zone" to achieve true and lasting change.

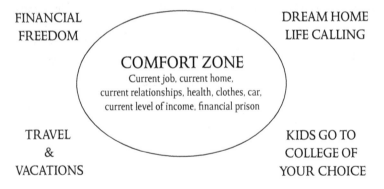

Everything currently in your life is inside your comfort zone; everything you want or aspire to have rests outside of your comfort zone. In order to obtain the things you desire, you must stretch your comfort zone until they fit, and the only way to do that is to do things that are uncomfortable or scary.

Let's look at this a different way. What makes up the circle? A line. Instead of thinking of this as a line, think of it as a *barrier*. To get what you want on the outside of your comfort zone, you must overcome your fears and break through the barrier.

Most people never break through these barriers. When most people experience fear, they stop, and as a result they stay in their comfort zone. Most people live their entire lives "comfortably miserable"; they aren't happy, they aren't living life to the fullest, but they do have the familiar and comfortable.

Your brain has a primary mission—survival. Therefore it does not want you to change because change is unknown and scary. So it will do its best to stop you from taking new actions, and in turn you stay right where you're at. We have all heard the stories or maybe know people involved in an abusive relationship that, against all logic, stay in that relationship. We watch from the outside shaking our heads. Even though these folks are not happy, they are comfortably miserable; taking action to improve their situation is simply too scary for them. Most people have an abusive or at least dysfunctional relationship with money, and I watch from the outside shaking my head because it doesn't make sense to me. Financial freedom is not harder than being in financial prison, IT'S JUST DIFFERENT!!! By simply doing a few different things, anyone can become financially free. That's exactly why we created our University, to not only teach but walk through it with you to create financial freedom. I know, though, that most people reading this will not attend the University; it's just too scary for them. They would rather stay comfortably miserable.

So much more is lost by inaction than wrong action. The problem is that inaction in day to day life usually doesn't have immediate consequence while wrong action usually does. If you didn't take action toward your financial freedom and the consequence of being retirement age and broke happened immediately, trust me, you would take the action. I say you don't have a day to waste. We are here in the grand scheme of things but for a blink of an eye, so make the best of it by taking massive action. When talking to several people in the latter years of their lives, I have found that they don't regret the things they have done, but instead the things they didn't do.

PART 4

Size Matters

Contributors

Following the explosion in that basement, I had literally hundreds of people who helped me recover: from doctors and nurses to physical therapists to family and friends. Their help was invaluable to putting me back in the game of life.

Guess what—this same concept applies to your financial freedom. You will need help. In fact, I say you'll need *lots* of help from others. No one is an island. During my business career before the explosion, and now on my mission following the accident to help as many others as possible achieve financial freedom, I've sought out and learned from dozens of the best authors, trainers, and speakers in the world. When I say size matters, I mean the size of your NETWORK. This includes all your relationships, business associates, mentors and trusted advisors. Your success depends on the size and quality of your network. It's not just about your network, but also how they view you. What is your reputation within your network?

Seek out people who will help you learn not just about business and finances, but about all aspects of life. And more importantly, "be the person" others would want to help and partner with.

That's what I did. And now I'm excited as heck to present here to you several of my friends (and one very special lady) who are literally experts in their particular area of expertise.

Earning a bunch of money is great, but you want to KEEP as much of that from the government as possible, right? Boom—check out Mr. Money -Mark Rothstein's chapter on taxes.

Building your nest egg is only the beginning—you want to protect your assets and make certain you and your family will be taken care of forever, right? Right! I'm honored to have Stewart Welch, III share his incredible asset protection insights with you.

What good is a bunch of money if you have a horrible relationship with the key people in your life, particularly your spouse? Check out Dino Watt's chapter on relationships; it's dynamite.

Finally, I've helped you obtain financial health...which is useless without PHYSICAL health. Melanie Nelson's chapter on health is one of the greatest gifts I can give you: her insights will not only change your thinking for the better, she'll help you add years to your life.

So please read on and enjoy. And in your own life, seek out and build key relationships from experts who can help you as these folks have helped me.

MARK ROTHSTEIN

Increase Your Tax IQ

Known to millions of radio listeners across the USA as "Mr. Money," Mark Rothstein is widely recognized as one of the country's top Certified Financial Planners and Income Tax Specialists. His career in personal finance and investment-related fields spans over 27 years. A graduate of Syracuse University, Mark is the Founder and President of TriStar Financial Services, one of the largest wealth management firms in Los Angeles. He has been featured on NBC nightly news and is a frequent guest commentator on Fox Business Channel. He was recognized as one of the top financial planners in the United States in both 2008 and 2009 by the Research Council of America, a respected peer review group for the financial industry. His number one passion in life is teaching people about their money: "Everybody can become educated and with this knowledge become rich," he says. He leads a three-day intensive money seminar. His students graduate with their entire financial life in order and structured for massive wealth creation. Visit his web site at www.mrmoneytalks.com

A Personal Note from Doug: *I have the privilege of calling Mark one of my personal friends and colleagues. He has a huge heart, a burning passion to help people, and the knowledge to back it up. He is the number one tax guy in the U.S., and what he shares with you here will be essential as you build your financial freedom. Check it out.*

The Tax hand - "Get out of My Pocket!"

One form of financial freedom comes from owning an ONGOING income business—one that "generates positive cash flow". Let me restate that last line to read…one that "**generates massive positive cash flow**".

Here's the catch.

Most business start-up's require cash/savings to purchase or create such a business. These businesses have expenses and of course generate income. One needs to purchase or build a business where the cash in-flow far *outweighs* the cash out-flow. Obviously, that's the key.

But, there's a problem.

Problem: The INTERNAL REVENUE SERVICE (lovingly referred to as the I.R.S.) TAXES your earned income or shall I more accurately say, *heavily* taxes your earned income. This is a problem because you need to save money, *after taxes*, to invest into your business.

Answer: PAY LESS TAXES.

The Internal Revenue Service is the income tax collection agency in the United States. This agency of the U.S. Government collects tax on your revenues on the federal level. Depending on what state or municipality you live—there may **also** be a "state" tax.

Each State has their own unique tax laws and structure as does the Federal Government. They publish their State tax rules and regulations and it is incumbent upon you to properly report your income and expenses on their forms and pay "your fair share" of taxes to them.

So, in most cases you have a 'double-wammy' of income taxes to pay. You are trying to keep your money yet the Fed's are taxing you, the States are taxing you, and NOW, there's even talk of a *new tax* called the VAT TAX (Value Added Tax).

We authors believe you are paying too much in taxes and it is time to pay fewer taxes and keep more of your earned money.

Here's how:

Find a **GREAT TAX PROFESSIONAL:**

Since when are you an expert in understanding all the tax laws and how to apply them? The Tax Code is 71,000 pages long. You should do what you do best and let tax experts do what they do best i.e. **your tax preparation**. Many people want to save a few hundred dollars in tax preparation fees by doing it themselves. Don't!! People say it's easy; you just need to follow the tax preparation program. Excuse me!! Just because you have tax software program does not mean you know what you are doing. The program only works based on your input. "But Mr. Money, it is such a wonderful program. It helps guide you, I can do it". Yep, it "certainly does" guide you... it guides you *to pay more taxes*. Don't!! Don't do it yourself.

REAL LIFE Example: I recently had a do-it-yourselfer call me. I agreed to help her as a favor to my friend. I understood her income and knew the proper way to report it, but we spent 20 minutes maneuvering "turbo tax" (country's largest tax software program) to produce the proper output onto the correct form line. It offered many different answers—all of them wrong and, coincidentally, it had the taxpayer paying an extra 15.3% in taxes. My 27 years of tax preparation – My understanding of the tax laws and *how to apply them* – That made the difference-not the software. Experience Counts.

Statistic: most taxpayers fail to take advantage of substantial tax deductions. In fact, according to IRS.gov, 1.3 Billion dollars of refunds are unclaimed each year.

Other benefits from having a tax professional on your side:

- You have peace of mind knowing your tax return was properly prepared.

- You have peace of mind knowing you took all the tax deductions you could and maximized your tax refunds.

- You have peace of mind knowing that the tax preparer signed their name on the tax return and will therefore defend your tax preparation in front of the IRS if you are ever audited.

Criteria to look for in choosing your tax expert

Key items to help guide you:

- Someone you like and you can relate to. Is a woman or a man a better choice for you? Does your gut tell you they are competent and they care about you?

- Someone who believes in paying the *least amount of taxes legally* is the best person. If they believe every taxpayer should pay their *fair share* of taxes and the rich do not pay enough, this may not be the one for you.

- Someone who prepares lots of tax returns and it is their main profession. You need someone with many years of experience that has prepared 1,000's of tax returns, not someone who prepares a few tax returns each tax season. Experience counts – especially in this profession.

- Someone who specializes in your tax area. If you are a business person and find a tax preparer who predominantly prepares taxes for retired individuals or specializes in non profit tax preparation – this is not the right person for you. Nope. Sorry. Get a tax preparer that specializes in *ongoing income businesses*. Believe me. This type of tax return, done correctly, has its own special tax rules, regulations and deductions. I know this. I specialize in this.

- Someone who specializes in tax preparation of your type of entity. If you are operating your business as an LLC (limited liability company) pick someone who specializes in this type of tax preparation. Or you operate as a Sub-S Corporation or a Schedule-C Sole Proprietorship. Get the tax person who understands these specific tax entities and associated forms and deductions.

- Someone who resides in your state. Remember, there may be state /municipality taxes due and again, you want someone that understands your states' specific tax regulations/laws.

- Someone who has the following credentials: CPA, EA or Tax Attorney (see Side Bar) These individuals have strict education and testing requirements to attain and maintain their credentials and therefore may be more competent and trustworthy.

Finding Your Tax Expert

One great way to find your tax expert is to ask your "successful" friends who they recommend. That is, ask your successful friends who have a business like yours.

You may also find your tax expert by going to: American Institute of Certified Public Accountants (www.AICPA.org), National Association of Enrolled Agents (www.NAEA.org), National Association of Tax Professionals (www.natptax.com) and the Section of Taxation of the American Bar Association (www.ABANET.org/tax).

Tax "Experts" to Avoid

Beware "expert" who offers you big tax refunds

Beware "expert" who charges you based on the amount of refunds or money saved

Beware "expert" who asks you to sign a blank tax return.

Beware your desire to save money by self-preparation. Again, do not do this!

Beware calling IRS for assistance. Only 64% of taxpayers who called the IRS during 2010 tax season reached a representative an NO, not all IRS answers were correct!

Anyone remember Timothy Geithner, United States Treasury Secretary? He endured public pummeling after lawmakers learned he had underpaid more than $34,000 in taxes while he was working for the International Monetary Fund. Geithner used "turbo tax" software (#1 largest tax software provider) to prepare his taxes and blamed his tax problems on "careless mistakes" not the tax software!!

Reminder: Your tax preparation fee is tax deductible, in the year you pay it (or charge on your credit card). Do not forget to deduct this fee. And, this fee is deductible on different forms in the tax return - which <u>does</u> make a difference on your total tax liability. Be sure your tax expert deducts this fee (and all fees) on the right tax forms so as to *maximize* your tax refund / *minimize* your tax liability.

How to help your tax expert:

The question is… What tax documents to keep? How to organize and maintain your tax (and financial) records? And what is tax deductible?

Becoming a Better Tax Manager

Make it your mission to help your tax preparer. Yes, you need an expert tax preparer on *your* team. But they can't shoulder the entire burden; you, too, must play an important role in minimizing your tax exposure. Why should you not arrange your financial affairs so you maximize your tax deductions and therefore insure the largest tax refunds… or better stated…arrange your affairs so you *pay the least amount of taxes*. You work hard to earn your **money** —its best to keep it!

Keep comprehensive, well organized documents.

For all business-relaxed expenses, keep your receipts. Keep these receipts organized, handy, and above all, in a place where you won't lose them! So, what exactly is business related and therefore what can be deducted? The Internal Revenue Code does not list what is and is not deductible. Instead Internal Revenue Code Section 162(a) simply says, "All ordinary and necessary expenses paid or incurred during the taxable year in carrying on a trade or business are deductible.

An ordinary expense is one that is common and accepted in a particular field of business, trade or profession."

"The facts and circumstances will determine if this expenditure was truly business or personal..." As you can see, **you** are the one who decides if it is business related. You and your tax preparer have to determine "was this an ordinary and necessary expense for my business?"

Here are some examples to help guide you:

A lavish and extravagant portion of business meal	0% deductible
Meal w/ customer, business discussed (before, during or after)	50% deductible
Meal with customer, no business discussed	0% deductible
Ticket price for sporting event, business discussed	50% deductible
Ticket price for sporting event, taxpayer does not attend	0% deductible
Scalper's premium for tickets	0% deductible
Transportation/lodging expenses while away from home on business	100% deductible

The examples can go on and on. Key point: have a discussion with your tax expert and have them educate you on what is and is not tax deductible. They also should coach you on what receipts to keep, which receipts to discard, and how long you should keep your receipts.

A few tips on IRS record retention:

The IRS has six years to audit your return if you underreport your gross income by 25% or more.

If the IRS believes you cheated on your taxes, it can audit you at any time. Similarly, if you don't file a tax return, the IRS can audit you in perpetuity.

If you deduct a loss from worthless securities, you should keep supporting documents for seven years.

Records for items that are subject to depreciation, such as equipment used for a business, should be kept for as long as the item is being depreciated. Depending on the item, that could be as long as seven years.

Documents related to real estate should be kept for as long as you own the property.

Great record keeping also pays another dividend—you'll feel safer and more in control should you ever get audited. I believe we should all get ready for increased scrutiny from the IRS. With U.S. government spending at record highs, they want—no, they **need**—your tax money to cover these costs. The government has instructed the IRS to collect more revenues. The agency is planning more audits, especially targeting taxpayers in the *highest tax brackets* and those who are *self-employed*. They have already successfully gone after foreign bank account holders maintaining off-shore, unreported bank accounts earnings.

The Rising Tide

What's more, income tax brackets are rising. Next year (2011) will bring a new higher Federal tax rate of 39.6% (vs. today's

36%), along with a capital gains tax (tax you pay on gain from sale of an asset) rate of 20% (vs. today's 15%). There also are additional "proposed tax cutbacks" targeted at the "rich" such as not allowing full charitable donation deductions, etc. **Additional taxes** are coming in 2013.

In 2013, there is the brand new Medicare-related tax – an increase of .9% levy on *high wage earners*. <u>And</u>, in 2013, a 3.8% Medicare Contribution Tax will be *imposed* on all unearned income of high-income individuals. This tax is on your interest, dividends, annuities, royalties, rents and **capital gain** sale of property (not personal home). Our future is ALL-ABOUT-MORE-TAXES! With rising tax rates – *more then ever* – keep comprehensive, well organized documents... especially business receipts.

Oh, one more thought on this, don't be fooled by "only the rich will pay more taxes"! With government spending gone amok, the government will need revenue from e-v-e-r-y-o-n-e. And, if you think you have escaped from the top tax bracket, watch as revenues decrease from "the rich" and more is needed…meaning YOU will be next to pay more.

Why?

In 2010 the national debt will approach $13 trillion—an amount equal to about 90% of America's GDP (gross domestic product) and about 50% higher than it's been any time in the last 20 years.

Obligations for Social Security, Medicare, Medicaid, Veterans' Benefits, and Pensions now stand at an *additional* $108 trillion over and above the "official" national debt.

Recently we added healthcare reform and that won't be free; plus, a new energy bill is around the corner. Who are we kidding?

WHERE is all this money going to come from? Oh, and what about the States and Municipalities around the country who are broke and have their hands out to Washington. I could go **on** *and* **on** *and* **on** about government deficit spending but you get the point. You...yes YOU...will be paying for all this. The rich in no-way-shape-or-form can pay enough taxes to cover all these expenses. Plus, (truth be told), the rich arrange their financial affairs to pay less/z-e-r-o- taxes; so again, this burden has to fall on someone. Hope it's not you.

Tax Reduction Strategies

Here are specific ways to begin to lower your tax burden. **Start early.** Many tax strategies to reduce your tax liability cannot be salvaged on December 31 - the last day of your tax period, or on April 15, when your tax return filing is due. You are too late. Decisions you make today can and will affect your tax bill next year and beyond. So, plan all your financial affairs now with taxes as a prime *consideration*. I did not say tax considerations are the **only** consideration but certainly should be a prime consideration. Every time in every circumstance if you pay less taxes you keep more of your money and that should be one of your key motivators. You win if you plan ahead. You lose if you do not plan or plan too late.

Be flexible. Life events can alter your overall financial picture and often your tax situation. Children are born, people change jobs or receive promotions, marriages and divorces occur, parents die, investments succeed and fail—these are all tax opportunities. Ask yourself, did you plan for these events and therefore arrange you tax/financial affairs to take maximum advantage? Or did you miss this opportunity?

Again, utilize a tax professional. Just like life changes constantly and requires constant adjustment, so do tax laws. You can bet your last dollar that every year—yes; I said every year, brings about new tax law changes. A good tax professional stays on top of these tax changes in order to help their clients plan ahead. Example, I just returned from an all day tax seminar. But it's July! Mr. Money, that's me, now has a jump ahead on the new tax law changes for next year. I can prepare my clients well in advance. Most tax preparers attend one update seminar in December. This is too late. Your tax year is over so it's too late to implement most tax strategies. Once you know the current laws (via your tax professional), you can then apply these to your personal tax situation. You do this well—you win, and you will pay minimal or even z-e-r-o taxes!

Location: Consider where you live. Seven states have **no income taxes**—Alaska, Florida, Nevada, South Dakota, Texas, Washington, and Wyoming. And, New Hampshire and Tennessee impose income tax only on interest and dividend earnings. Living in any of these states will lower your tax burden. When thinking tax reduction, consider these states to **live in** or these states to **retire to.**

Furthermore, factor in Social Security and Pensions. If you are considering living in a state that does not impose an income tax, you'll also want to know how it taxes social security and pensions, since a major part of retirement income is earned from these sources... particularly pension plan distributions. By now, you don't want to count on this alone for your retirement, and if you apply what you read in this book you won't have to. Social Security income is completely *exempt from tax* in 27 states: Alabama, Arizona, Arkansas, California, Delaware, Georgia, Hawaii, Idaho, Illinois, Indiana, Kentucky, Louisiana, Maine, Maryland, Massachusetts, Michigan, Mississippi, New Jersey, New York, North Carolina,

Ohio, Oklahoma, Oregon, Pennsylvania, South Carolina, Virginia, and Wisconsin (and the District of Columbia).

Of the states with an income tax, 36 fully or partially *exempt* pension income. Only California, Indiana, Nebraska, Rhode Island, and Vermont do not. In these states you pay in full. As you can see, each state has its particular state tax attributes - all are different. Some states exempt public pensions from taxation but tax private pensions, or exempt public pensions earned in that state but not public pensions earned in another state. Yes my head hurts too and it is shaking back and forth as I'm sure yours is too. Do not be overwhelmed. It's my job to know this and help you with it; I hope your Tax Expert does too! So simply ask your great tax preparer to find out how this state taxes you; since you are thinking of moving there.

Timing: All the above is written to give you a hint of what is needed to become tax-wise, both during your prime earning years and in your retirement years. Always, every year there are tax planning moves to make—do you make them? Did you get tax knowledge? Did you hire a tax expert with the knowledge and have <u>planning</u> meetings (not just one meeting)

An expert tax person who is also an expert financial planner is the ULTIMATE PROFESSIONAL to hire and have in your corner. $$$

STEWART WELCH, III

Asset Protection

Stewart is the author of several books, including The Complete Idiot's Guide to Getting Rich, *J.K. Lasser's* New Rules for Estate & Tax Planning, *and the* 10 Minute Guide to Personal Finances for Newlyweds. *His financial expertise has drawn national attention and he is often sought out by the national media for his opinions. He has appeared on CNN , CNBC and Fox News as well as hosting his own show, "Welch Profiles: Personal Success Stories" where he interviewed such notables as legendary investor and author Jimmy Rogers and Stephen Forbes, Editor of Forbes magazine. He has been quoted in, among other publications, The Wall Street Journal, Money, Forbes, Kiplinger, The New York Times, Smart Money and Worth. You can find out more about Stewart by visiting his website at www. GetRichOnPurpose.com .*

A Personal Note from Doug: *It is an honor to call Stewart my friend and colleague; he is the epitome of class and is a true southern gentleman. He has a list of accomplishments and credentials that make him blush. The information he shares here is essential to protecting what you create financially.*

Once you've got it, you'll need to protect it!

We have a litigation crisis here in America. Our mantra: "Sue everybody and we'll sort it out later." It is estimated that there are more than 1 million lawyers in America...one for every 300 citizens. What are the chances of you getting sued sometime during your lifetime? Turns out, they're pretty good. In fact, some research suggests that you'll be involved in an average of *five* lawsuits during your lifetime.

What are your odds, personally, of being a victim of a lawsuit? Take a moment now to complete our **Personal Liability Exposure Quiz:**

Personal Liability Exposure Quiz

Circle your answer to each of the following questions:

1. Y N Do you have full or part ownership in a business?

2. Y N Do you own real estate other than your primary residence?

3. Y N Are you a member of a 'high lawsuit risk' profession such as a physician?

4. Y N Do you have dependant children who are of driving age?

5. Y N Do you generally talk on your phone while driving on more than a incidental basis?

6. Y N Do you ever text on your phone while driving?

7. Y N Does your home have a swimming pool?

8. Y N Would people 'guess' that you are wealthy based on your home, cars, clothes, or outward lifestyle?

9. Y N Do you ever drink alcohol and drive a vehicle?

10. Y N Does your net worth exceed $1 million?

SCORE: _____ Total number of 'Yes' answers.

8-10 Liability exposure is very <u>high</u>. Consider working with a professional who specializes in Asset Protection Strategies.

4-7 Liability Exposure is <u>moderate</u>. Consider taking measures to protect your most important financial assets.

0-3 Liability exposure is <u>low</u>. Consider the balance between costs, time and benefit to implement an Asset Protection Strategy.

© 2010 T.E.A.M. Worldwide

How did you score? Like most people, you probably have at least a moderate risk of getting sued. With this in mind, wouldn't it make sense to develop an asset protection strategy?

The topic of asset protection is both broad and deep; creating an effective strategy is a bit like peeling an onion…in reverse! I'll begin with basic strategies, and then move through more complex strategies that are typically implemented as your net worth, and liability risks, grow. For each strategy, I'll outline the issue, solutions, and give you the 'Action' you should consider. Remember, the Universe Rewards ACTION and in the case of Asset Protection, it may just save your ASSets!

LIFESTYLE

Monitor your lifestyle. At the most basic level, your lifestyle can either minimize or elevate your risks of a lawsuit. Some of the obvious things would include not drinking and driving, observing speed limits, securing a fence around your pool, etc. For example, research proves that talking on the phone while driving is the equivalent of driving while slightly intoxicated; driving while texting is even worse—it's considered the equivalent of driving while drunk! Once while sitting in my car at a red light, a young lady using her cell phone scraped my bumper. While no one was hurt, the damage to my car was still $1,200, and the cost of repairing her car, I suspect, was much more. Had there been injuries, she would have opened herself up for a lawsuit that would have been difficult to defend.

Action Recommended: After completing our quiz, take a moment to think about how you can reduce lawsuit risks related to your lifestyle.

INSURANCE

Insurance as your first line of defense. A number of years ago, a client and his family were driving to the airport in Denver, Colorado, after a week of snow skiing. On this beautiful sunny day with clear roads, he suddenly hit a patch of ice. The car slid into the oncoming lane in the direct line-of-traffic of another car, and the two cars collided. Fortunately for my client, he and his family had buckled up and were not injured. Unfortunately, the two young ladies in the other car had not buckled up. Both came crashing through the windshield, causing severe facial lacerations. They sued and won a judgment in excess of $700,000. If my client's auto liability coverage had been, say $50,000, where would the young ladies' attorney gone to satisfy the balance of the judgment? That's right—his personal assets. Fortunately, we had wrapped his auto and homeowners insurance with a $1 million Umbrella Liability Policy.

In my experience, most people do not carry umbrella liability coverage, yet it's perhaps one of the least expensive and most effective ways to shield your assets from a lawsuit. An umbrella liability policy typically has a very large deductible, say $300,000 or $500,000, but then covers any liability that arises from an auto or homeowners claim up to $1 million above the deductible. In order to avoid having a 'gap' in coverage, you'll need to make certain that your auto and homeowner's coverage limits are equal to your umbrella policy's deductible.

Action Recommended: Meet with your property and casualty agent and have him or her add an umbrella liability policy for a minimum of $1 million. This policy often costs less than $300 per year (though you may have to increase coverage for your auto and homeowners insurance as well).

For our clients, we do a Liability Risk Assessment whereby we attempt to determine if there are any obvious liability risks that need to be addressed with a particular strategy. I have had people tell me that they are not concerned about liability because if they feel threatened, they'll simply transfer assets out of their name. This won't work because of the federal **'fraudulent transfers rule'** that states that funds transferred in an attempt to avoid creditors is illegal, and the court will order that the transaction be reversed and the funds be turned over to the creditors.

<u>**Professional Liability Insurance**</u>. If you own a business, you'll want to have professional liability coverage which may come in a variety of forms, including malpractice insurance (doctors, lawyers, and other professionals), errors and omissions, product

liability, and premises liability coverage. From time to time, you may be asked to serve on various boards of either non-profit or for-profit organizations...often serving with little or no pay. This can be very dangerous to your wealth. Generally, I recommend avoiding such appointments. If you are considering joining a board, make certain that the group has significant Officers and Directors Liability Insurance. Remember, as a director, you are liable for the misdeeds of the people who are running the organization, and rarely do you have access to much information about their activities. I have a personal friend who forfeited hundreds of thousands of dollars after the board on which he served received a multimillion dollar judgment.

Action Recommended: Get with an insurance agent who specializes in commercial insurance and have him or her do a complete insurance review with particular emphasis on liability coverage.

One of the weaknesses of using insurance as your defense against lawsuit is that you will lose control over your defense. In other words, your insurance company will pick the lawyer whose *primary* job is to represent the insurance company...not you. Often they will settle a claim rather than pursue it even if you have done nothing wrong. This can be particularly troublesome if the suit involves your reputation. Your best solution may be to hire your own attorney to do a case review at key junctures along the way and interact with the insurance company attorneys.

Life Insurance: From an asset protection perspective, one of the mistakes I see people make is to, inadvertently or otherwise, name their 'estate' as the beneficiary of their life insurance. I was brought in on a case where the husband had died leaving $1 million of life insurance payable to his 'estate'. To complicate matters, he did not have a will, which meant the laws of his state of residence decided how the insurance proceeds would be distributed. The result was that $500,000 went outright to the widow (no asset protection!) and $500,000 was held under a state conservatorship for their nine-year-old son until he turned 19, at which time he'd receive his money, including all the growth, outright. I'm guessing you can see the problem here. The widow, on the verge of a nervous breakdown, had to sell their home and, because she had been out of the workplace for more than a decade, she took a low-paying job just to pay the bills.

Naming an individual as the beneficiary protects the insurance proceeds from lawsuits against the insured.

Action Recommended: Make certain that your life insurance has a named beneficiary for asset protection.

FEDERAL & STATE LAW

Both federal and state laws provide a variety of protections that are vital for you to know about and consider taking advantage of to protect your assets from lawsuit.

Federal Exemptions: Federal law protects all assets held in certain retirement plans, including company sponsored profit sharing, 401(k), 403b, and pension plans (Employee Retirement Income Security Act-ERISA). In addition, in a law passed in 1995 (Bankruptcy Abuse Prevention and Consumer Protection Act), Individual Retirement Accounts (IRAs) are exempt from creditors for up to $1 million if the owner files for bankruptcy protection. Assets rolled over from a qualified plan, such as a company retirement plan to your personal IRA, do not count towards this $1 million limitation and remain fully protected from a law suit.

Action Recommended: Consider shielding assets by investing through retirement plans. If you want to invest primarily in alternative investments such as real estate, oil and gas, or non-public business enterprises, consider setting up a self-directed IRA. You'll need a custodian who specializes in these types of accounts.

<u>State Exemptions.</u> Each state has its own set of exemptions laws that provide a varying level of protection of assets from bankruptcy.

Action Recommended: Become familiar with your state laws for exemptions available to you. For a state-by-state summary, visit the Resource Center at **www.GetRichOnPurpose.com** and click on 'State-by-State Bankruptcy Exemption Laws'.

TITLING OF ASSETS

The way most people title their assets does little to protect them in the event of a legal judgment. The three worst ways to own property, from an asset protection point of view, are in your own name, joint ownership, or in a partnership.

<u>Owning assets in your name</u>: The main advantages include simplicity and flexibility, but you have absolutely no protection from a lawsuit.

<u>Joint ownership of assets</u>: Joint ownership actually *increases* your risks of fallout from a lawsuit. For example, if you own an apartment building with your friend and he received a judgment unrelated to the apartments, his creditors could force the sale of the property or become your partner…their choice! If they choose to force a sale of the apartments, you will receive your share but the timing of sale could produce poor financial results.

Owning assets in a partnership: It may not seem possible, but owning assets in a partnership may increase your liability exposure more than ownership in your own name or joint ownership! This is because in a partnership, it's possible for you to be held legally responsible for the misdeeds of one of your partners! Not only could the creditor take his share of any partnership assets, but they can come after your share of partnership assets as well. Under certain circumstances, the creditor can breach the partnership and seize personal assets.

Action Recommended: Rethink how you hold title to your assets. While you have a number of good options, perhaps the best choice is a **Limited Liability Company,** or LLC. Easy and inexpensive to set up and easy to maintain, an LLC is treated as a separate entity or 'person' from a legal perspective. This means that assets held within your LLC are segregated from other assets and cannot be seized by creditors for a judgment not related directly to that LLC. Alternatively, if there is a judgment related directly to that LLC, while the LLC's assets are exposed, assets outside the LLC are not. Thus consider creating, as needed, multiple LLC's to 'segregate' assets from each other. For example, you may want one LLC to hold your 'risky' assets such as a rental property, boats, airplanes, recreational vehicles, and so on, and another to hold your 'safe' assets such as your personal investment accounts, jewelry, and antiques.

Beyond the LLC, the most popular choice of legal entity for asset protection is the **Family Limited Partnership,** or FLP. FLP's are typically more complex and expensive to set up and manage than LLC's but also offer some additional advantages including possible reduction of estate taxes. There are also **Domestic Asset Protection Trusts** and **Foreign Asset Protection Trusts** which are sometimes used by wealthy families or those whose occupation places them at greater risks, such as physicians. While beyond the scope of this chapter, these topics are covered in my book, *J.K. Lasser's New Rules for Estate & Tax Planning*.

Protecting your home: Protecting your home against lawsuit may be a bit of a challenge because most couples hold title to their home under 'joint tenants with rights of survivorship.' This means that if one spouse dies, the home automatically transfers to the surviving spouse without going through probate. Yes, it's simple, but exposes what, for most people, is their most valuable asset to lawsuit. To complicate matters, most states provide homeowners a 'Homestead Exemption' which significantly reduces property taxes. If you were to transfer title into a trust, or LLC, you'd likely no longer be eligible for the exemption...a high price to pay over the life of your home. Most mortgages also have a 'due on sale' clause that requires you to pay off your mortgage should you transfer title out of your name. Here are some possible strategies:

1. If you are in an occupation considered 'risky' from a lawsuit perspective, such as a physician, you could transfer title to your spouse. If you receive a judgment against you that exceeds your insurance limits, your home would be protected. One weakness is that there is no protection against judgments directly against your spouse. Another weakness is that in the event of a divorce, some courts will view ownership as '9/10's of the law'... meaning your spouse might get the house while you get stuck with the debt!

2. You could take out a large loan against your home and invest the proceeds (your equity) in one or more of the strategies discussed in this chapter. In effect, your home

is now much less valuable and less of a target of would-be creditors. The weakness here is that you must make large mortgage payments.

3. In my book, *J.K. Lasser's New Rules for Estate & Tax Planning*, I discuss a little-known titling for married couples called, "Cross Contingent Remainder Deeds." Available in some states, this prevents creditors from forcing the sale of your home unless the judgment is against *both* spouses.

Action Recommended: While protecting your home may be a challenge, it's probably also your most valuable asset, and hence worth the energy and effort needed to protect it to the fullest. Consider whether one or more of the above strategies would be appropriate and seek advice from a qualified professional advisor.

LEGAL DOCUMENTS

Legal documents are another way to protect your assets. Three primary categories you should consider include: legacy planning, prenuptial agreements, and hold-harmless agreements.

<u>**Legacy Planning:**</u> When I review the wills of new clients, the documents often leave assets outright to the surviving spouse or, if there is no surviving spouse, to the children at a young age, say 21 or 25. A transfer directly to the surviving spouse continues to subject those assets to a potential lawsuit. As for the children, outright distributions at a young age expose assets to two risks. First, in my experience, many people in their twenties are ill-equipped to handle large sums of money, and will either spend the money or invest it poorly. Second, the divorce rate in America continues to hover above 50%. Leaving your assets directly to children can expose those assets to a future divorce. Combine the odds of a divorce with the odds of a lawsuit during an adult child's

lifetime, and you can easily see the importance of developing an asset protection strategy. In our practice, we developed a concept we call, "Legacy Trust with Asset Protection Attributes." With this, the clients' assets at death are transferred to a trust for the benefit of the surviving spouse or children for their lifetime. They receive monthly cash flow from the trust as well as principal distributions for predetermined events or situations such as education, health, down payment for the purchase of a home, and so on. Should the trust beneficiary be threatened by a divorce or lawsuit, the trust language shields trust assets.

Action Recommended: Take a moment to determine the total value of your estate including life insurance. Review your will to determine how your assets will be left to your heirs, then decide if a Legacy Trust is a strategy worth considering.

Prenuptial Agreements: I'm sure you're all familiar with the concept of a prenuptial agreement whereby couples, prior to being married, sign an agreement limiting the transfer of assets should the couple later divorce. While most typical where one or the other (or both) of the couple have children by a previous marriage, we also have used a prenuptial agreement in cases where a child is expected to inherit substantial assets either outright or in the form of a family business interest.

Action Recommended: If you or one of your children is contemplating marriage, consider the advisability of a prenuptial agreement. While this can be an awkward conversation between the marrying couple, it has roughly a 50% chance of turning out to be one of the most wealth-preserving conversations of your life! I suggest having this conversation as early as possible (rather than shortly before the wedding). We often advise our clients to let us be the 'bad-guy' for having 'required' a prenuptial agreement. You may want to employ a similar strategy.

Hold-Harmless Agreements: A hold-harmless agreement is an agreement between two parties where one party agrees to 'defend' the other party should a lawsuit arise out of a specific set of circumstances. For example, if you were contemplating buying a company, you might require the seller provide a hold-harmless agreement whereby the seller would both defend you and your company against any lawsuits that arise out of acts that occurred prior to your ownership. Any judgments as a result of the lawsuit would be the responsibility of the seller.

Action Recommended: Before entering into any business deal, be sure to protect yourself from 'unknown' and 'unknowable' lawsuits whose origin is related to the seller by insisting on a hold-harmless agreement. The weakness of this strategy is that the agreement is only as good as the assets or insurance of the seller.

CONCLUSION

We've covered a lot of ground regarding asset protection; it would be easy for you to get overwhelmed and do nothing. As a result, at some time in the future, you may find yourself in a situation in which you wish you had taken action. Consider approaching asset protection one of two ways:

View it as a process whereby you create 'building blocks' of asset protection. Start by listing all of your assets and liabilities on a piece of paper. (For a form, visit the Resource Center at www. GetRichOnPurpose.com and click on Asset/Liability Review.) Decide what assets you feel need protecting now, and begin with the simplest and least expensive strategy. As you acquire additional assets, you'll revise and update your strategy periodically.

Work with a professional who has asset protection expertise. This could be a financial advisor, attorney, or an accountant. In most cases, you'll need the assistance of an attorney to transfer titles, set up trusts or perform other legal maneuvers.

Implement a plan customized to your situation BEFORE you need one. You will be glad that you did and you can thank me later.

DINO WATT

Relationships and Money

Dino Watt has always had a passion for improving marriages, but his mission really ignited in 2006 while working as a success coach. That year he was awarded Coach of the Year by the Enlightened Wealth Institute. Many of his students were married couples trying to start or grow a business. In his coaching sessions, Dino noticed how frequently couples struggled to effectively work together in their business. This realization gave him the opportunity to teach his clients how to incorporate specific systems into their business, and more importantly, marriage. Soon couples were achieving the success they desired as a result of Dino's individual coaching. It was through this feedback and encouragement that Dino created The Business of Marriage training program. Dino and his wife, Shannon, recently celebrated their 15th wedding anniversary. They have three children, ages 12, 10 and 9 years old.

A Personal Note from Doug: *When I first met Dino, my impression of him was this: here's a calm, cool, collected and content dude. These impressions still stand today after having known him for several years. Dino practices what he teaches and it shows on him how well it works. He is a master coach and teacher. His expertise is necessary for everyone because you cannot have money without relationships or relationships without money.*

In a recent study by the Institute for Marriage and Public Policy, researchers found that the cost of fragmented (divorced and unwed childbearing) families on the U.S. taxpayer is $112 billion a year. That's billion with a "B" coming out of your wallet. Over one decade, that calculates to more than $1 trillion. However, if the rate of fragmented families was reduced by just 1 percent, taxpayers would save more than $1.1 billion annually. There's an old saying that no one really cares about something until it affects their own pocketbook. If that's what it takes really takes for people to start wanting to do something about this huge problem, then that study should get a lot of people thinking about their marriage in a whole other light.

One area widely overlooked when it comes to the importance of successful and happy marriages is the business world. In the past decade or so, major companies have allocated financial resources on "team building" outings and trainings in order to build a sense of togetherness, loyalty and dedication among co-workers. They do have a somewhat hidden motive: an increase in team work will, in almost all cases, increase employee productivity rates, too. The component most companies still miss, however, is the importance of a successful marriage and family life at home.

A few years ago my wife and I began investing in real estate. After about a year, one of the largest real estate investment education promoters in the country recruited me to coach for them. Within a year I was voted the company's coach of the year.

During my coaching sessions, I began to notice something very interesting regarding my married students. I began to notice their biggest roadblock to success wasn't the market, the many different types of ways to do real estate, or even the desire to work hard. No, their major road block was simply each other! They got in each other's way instead of building on the other's strengths. I found I spent most of my time during their sessions advising them on how to set up systems so that they could work together both in and out of the business.

One day one of my married students suggested that I start a coaching program based on those systems and practices. I thought this was a great idea, so to begin I took those systems and practices and compared them to how successful companies run their business. It made me realize how much a marriage is just like a business, and that if we took some of those same systems and applied them to marriage, we, as a country might see better success.

Now I understand some might say referring to marriage as a business seems a bit cold, unloving, or impersonal, so I want to clarify if I may.

I believe that successful businesses are successful because they have specific systems in place that helped them on their road to success.

I also believe that the most important business in the world is marriage and family. However, far too often people get into a marriage without specific systems in place to insure their success.

So here is the million dollar question when it comes to the argument against using successful business practices and systems as a comparison to a successful marriage:

If systems are good enough for creating a successful business, why wouldn't systems also be good enough for creating successful marriages?

Most people want to be successful in business. They don't typically start one with the idea of failing in mind. It's the same with marriage. People get married with the desire to succeed. Most sane people don't get married with the idea of failing in mind.

The challenge is this: in business, you usually are going to start with things like a written plan, something to show others everything from why this is a good business to get involved with to financial projections of success. In marriage, however, very few people have a written plan as to their reasons why marrying each other is a good idea or what their projection of success looks like to them. I'm convinced that if more people looked at their marriage as a business and created systems they can refer to and rely on through the years, there would be far fewer divorces in the world.

WARNING

You might want to discount the information as "too simple" or "obvious". To that I would ask one question: How has what you've been doing so far been working for you? These ideas and systems have been put together through study, life experience, and a true desire to help. There is a reason you are being given this information. You or someone you know needs it and will benefit greatly by adhering to these ideas and thoughts.

Putting the Systems in Place

A happy and successful marriage is the genesis of true success in and out of the workplace. Whether you are a coal miner or the CEO of a Fortune 500 company, any employee happy at home will become more successful in their profession. On-the-job happiness and success comes from knowledge that the employee's spouse is supportive, encouraging, proud, and interested in their spouse's success. If more companies invested more time and resources to making sure their employees' homes had the support and resources they need to overcome challenges and turbulent times in their personal lives, there would be far less divorces in this country.

However, we are all responsible for ourselves and our own happiness. In other words, we can't rely on our employers or business colleagues (if we own a business). The following systems are some easy ways to create a successful business. When you put these practical applications to work in your marriage, you will see a dramatic difference in your personal AND professional life.

Tough Recruiting Process- *Marriage is more enjoyable than dating!*

Companies that want to grow and become successful don't hire just anyone. They have a tough and challenging recruitment process. They look for the best person, someone who will both do the job and help the company grow and meet its targets.

Why is it that people generally say, "dating is fun" and, "marriage is tough"? In reality, shouldn't these be the exact opposite? Dating with the purpose of finding a life-long spouse is a rigorous process and finding a compatible person who shares your values and targets, that's the hardest part. On the other hand, once you've committed to someone and have successful systems in place to nurture the relationship, that's when the real fun should begin.

I enjoy looking at the business structure of companies like Google, Microsoft, and Pixar Animation. If you walk into the doors of those companies, you will see people rolling along on scooters, people in casual clothes having fun, all the while being highly productive. The owners of these companies believe that finding the best people for the job and giving them the freedom to have fun and be creative while working towards a common target allows employees to be their best. I don't think anyone can argue against the success of these and other companies like them.

Team Building-*Continual courting*

Successful companies know that employees who enjoy their environment will build strong relationships with each other through creative work and off-site activities, thus producing more value for the company.

What's the marriage equivalent? I say continual dating, vacations, and alone time are musts! The number one reason sited for no-fault divorce is that "we just grew apart". I guarantee you that if you do these three things on a consistent and regular basis, you will not grow apart!

Dating and spending time together with your spouse is one of the most important, if not *the* most important, thing you can do to strengthen your relationship. When I say spend time with each other, I don't mean sitting in front of the television not talking. I mean taking walks together, going to a dance class together, riding bikes together, just sitting and talking together, and so on. Get creative. Keep up on the dating process. Open the car door for her. Get made up for him. (We'll touch on marketing and advertising to each other in a minute.) The point of dating is to remind each other on a consistent basis why you chose each other—to grow together.

The only way to keep in touch with each other is to be in touch with each other. While time with the family is definitely important; time with each other is vital. The time you spend developing your relationship and continuously falling in love over and over again will be a huge teaching tool for your children that they will hopefully emulate in their lives.

Evaluations- *Reconnecting on a daily basis*

Progress reports and evaluations are essential for any growing company. This allows upper management to see where the company is, where it is going, and what needs to be worked on. Every marriage also needs daily come-together time, with no distractions, to talk about the household. This is not a whine session, it is a constructive update.

A good time to implement this is during "pillow talk." I like pillow talk for two reasons. One, it forces the two of you to go to bed together at the same time. If in your relationship one of you consistently goes to bed while the other one is watching television or on the computer, you are missing out on your time to reconnect, the time to recharge each others' love batteries, the time to really check in with each other. Second, if you do talk in the dark, which I recommend, you can talk with each other without dealing with facial expressions, which can sometimes be misconstrued. This allows you to get your point out or your request voiced without the challenge of reading something in the other's face about what you have said.

Here are some topics I suggest that you discuss (as appropriate):

- Summary of your day

- Good things that transpired

- Challenges that need to be addressed

- What's going on tomorrow

- Things needed for house or each other

- Discipline and praise needed for kids

- Any miscellaneous topic not suitable for discussion in front of the kids

Marketing/ Advertising- Keeping the spark alive

Picture walking into a doctor's office and there were dust webs in the corners of the walls, filth on the floor, the paint on the walls was old and chipping off, the furniture in the lobby looked broken down and smelled bad, the magazines were all from 10 years ago, and the doctor told you that he doesn't believe in going to classes to update his skills because, "If it was good enough then, it's good enough now."

Ladies: Would you want that doctor as your OBGYN?

Guys: Would you want him for your prostate exam?

Businesses that don't keep up with the latest trends or continually market to their customer base will not be in business for very long. Finding new clients is only part of the battle. Long-term retention of loyal clients is also a key to a company's ultimate success.

During the dating process, both parties usually do everything they can to attract the other sex. Too often, once the "catch" has been caught, one (or both) spouses begin to relax their appearance. Now that they are in a long-term relationship, maintaining a fabulous outward appearance doesn't seem to be such a high priority. This is backwards to how it should be. It makes more sense to look our best for the one we love, not for that blind date we'll never see again. I believe that it's each spouse's responsibility to take care of them selves physically, mentally, and spiritually so they are always bringing their best self to the marriage.

The doctor's office example is also relevant to your home. In my real estate business, I have seen my fair share of lived-in homes. It always surprises me when I walk into a home that hasn't been taken care of—not in a need-to-fix-the-sink type of way, but in a hey, why don't we throw anything anywhere and not pick up after ourselves way. If you don't care about your home's upkeep and care, doesn't this spill over into your romantic life with your spouse? You bet! The home should be a sanctuary from the outside world for you and your family. However, if it resembles the doctor's office I mentioned previously, the desire to return will also be diminished.

This is especially true in the bedroom. I have seen master bedrooms where the most intimate and loving parts of relationships are supposed to take place that look more like a storage unit than a place of love and togetherness. The marriage bed should be warm and inviting, a place you and your spouse feel comfortable sharing with each other. It shouldn't be a place of darkness and despair. If you have to move the pile of old clothes or brush off the crumbs from your bed in order to get into it, something is wrong.

Please note that I'm *not* saying that a home should be spotless and free of clutter or dirt at all times. Believe me, I lived in that house growing up with my parents and there was definitely no correlation between the house and my parents staying together. The point is that your home needs to be a place where love and joy can flourish, not a place where junk and dirt are allowed to suppress your full feelings for one another. It's all part of the marketing process.

Remember:

Marketing is all about getting the attention of your audience.

Advertising is all about making them want what you got.

Hostile Take Over- *Children and the dynamic they bring*

Successful businesses know beforehand what their plan of action will be when handling an insubordinate employee, or if faced with a larger company wanting to buy them out. Unfortunately, kids don't come with a company handbook!

Discipline and rewards for kids should be discussed well before kids are born. Once they arrive, family rules and consequences should be clearly explained. Consistent follow through is imperative, as is maintaining a "united front" among the parents. Nothing sabotages a marriage quicker than when one parent undermines the other in front of their children.

It should be well understood by everyone involved that Mom and Dad's relationship with each other is the number one priority of the family, and that kids, while extremely important, take second priority. The moment either spouse emotionally places a child before the other, spousal problems will arise.

"Problems become Challenges"- *Reframing a situation to be a positive.*

When Fortune 500 companies run into financial or company issues, you never hear the CEO say they are having "problems." Instead, they refer to "challenges" to be faced. The CEO will then discuss how the company will overcome or rise to the challenge.

When we reframe what we would normally call a problem and make it a challenge, it becomes something your mind recognizes as merely an obstacle you can overcome and ultimately win. Problems send most people into fear mode, and can paralyze many into inaction. However, if we view problems as challenges, our brain immediately begins working on solutions. Our subconscious then becomes empowered to help us work through it and overcome the challenge.

For the next week, I want you to do this: Every time you want to say the word *problem*, use the word *challenge* instead. I promise you will have a better outlook on the situation

Currency

In the book the *Five Love Languages,* author Gary Chapman explains his philosophy on how we show our love to one another through five different languages. In business we definitely use language, but more importantly we use currency. For your relationship, let's discover your spouse's emotional currency.

In business, we use currency to measure success. There are many types of currency, of course. The United States uses the dollar, Japan the Yen, Europe the Euro, and so forth. All businesses, even non-profit organizations, need money to operate. When companies decide to do business with each other internationally, it is vital they know the exchange rate for their primary currency, as well as the rate of the currency they will be doing business with. (Lately, the dollar's value has been dropping internationally, so it typically takes a lot more of them to buy something overseas than it did before. That is not to say there is no value in it from other countries; it just might not be the currency other businesses consider the most valuable to them.)

In your marriage, your spouse and you both have one currency you value above another—how we express or show love to one another. This currency communicates your love to them and theirs to you. The challenge arises in many marriages when either one THINKS or ASSUMES they know the other's currency without actually taking the time to find out, or better yet, *ask* what their spouse's real currency is. For example, some people highly value physical touch over material gifts, while others place the most value on together time.

Confusion happens because while all currency has some value, not all currency has the *most* value according to each person. A service project is probably always appreciated by her, but if her most valued currency is encouragement or praise, you will never get the response you want, and she will never feel you are as loving as you could be in her mind.

This becomes evident when you hear someone say things like, "I do everything on the list of honey-do's! I take out the trash, she never has to clean the car or mow the lawn, and yet it is still never enough!" Even though those things are nice, if all she really wants is for you to tell her how beautiful she is, how proud you are of her, and how amazing a mother she is, you will be coming up short in her emotional currency "bank." It's as if you are giving her $1,000 U.S., yet her currency is YEN. She appreciates the money and knows it has value; it just isn't the currency she prefers.

All of us have a currency that we value over all others; most of the time ours is not the same as our spouses. In other words, our "exchange rates" are not equal. The good news is there are only five currencies you have to learn. As soon as you know your spouse's primary currency, you can focus on providing that. You will then see a major difference in how they accept your tokens of affection.

Here they are:

- *Un-paid overtime* (charity or service). Doing something for them, even when you don't want to. This is my wife's. She feels the most love from me when I hang a picture, clean out a closet, paint a room, run errands, or just about anything on my eternal "honey-do" list.

- *Healthy handshake or pat on the back* (physical touch). Holding hands, a hug, sitting next to each other, a back rub, a tap on the bum, sexual foreplay, and sexual intercourse.

- *Acknowledgement of a job well done* (encouragement, praise). Telling your spouse how wonderful they are, celebrating a "win" at work, encouraging them to peruse a hobby or education, telling them how proud you are of them, telling them how good they look and make you feel, tell her what a great mother/wife she is, tell him how much you appreciate his hard work.

- *Bonus pay/ Company Trip.* Cards, flowers, presents, love letters, making dinner for him/her, and gifts both handmade and store bought.

- *Private mentoring.* Talking with each other (television off, or at least on pause), running errands together, going on dates, going for walks together, vacations, playing games with the kids.

As you can see, all of these currencies have a value to them. However, we all hold one value over the other. If you figure out what your spouse's primary love currency, and focus on giving them this currency, you will never feel short changed!

A Final Note

In whatever business venture you choose in order to create your own economy, remember this simple truth: You can become the most successful business person in the world, but if your success comes at the detriment of your marriage, you will be the poorest person in the world. One of my favorite quotes comes from a mentor of mine, David McKay, who sums it up this way:

"No other success can compensate for failure in the home."

MELANIE NELSON

A Healthy You

After graduating top of her class Melanie built a very successful practice working in the Health Industry. She worked with clients such as top professional athletes and teaching health classes to those who desired a higher level of vitality; many of these people suffering from chronic diseases. A mentor and example to many, she changed her own life around, trained for and completed a triathlon, raised tens of thousands of dollars for Charities and has trained internationally for one of the largest personal and financial growth companies. She is a woman who at a young age has never shied away from a challenge and because of that has achieved many "firsts". Creating her first level of financial freedom at the age of 26, and achieving her target of personally becoming a Millionaire by age 30; she is now the President of Ignite Promotions. Melanie is known for saying; *"The only difference between your dreams and making them a reality is a plan of action and sticking to it".* Melanie is an advocate for people who want to help themselves reach new levels. She still helps people today achieve their own "firsts".

A Personal Note from Doug: *When I first met Melanie, she had a sales pitch for me. I knew then that she was a go-getter. She has a no nonsense approach and is full of fire. I also knew she was the love of my life, and a couple years later married her. Shortly after I met Melanie, I began incorporating her health advice and to this day people who have not seen me in awhile come up to me telling me how amazing I look and are amazed at how much energy and endurance I have. This information is transformational!*

> *"So many people spend their health gaining wealth, and then have to spend their wealth to regain their health."*
>   - A.J. Reb Materi

Health is the great equalizer of men and women. Let me prove it. If you had a heart attack on the street and had trouble breathing, I guarantee you this: you would *pray* that the homeless person smelling like urine with the teeth rotting and falling out (the one you would normally avoid) had the presence of mind to come over and do CPR on you! Another great example is the movie "The Bucket List" where a multi-billionaire shares the same hospital room—and disease—with a humble man with a comfortable existence, and because of this connection they share an incredible journey together.

I am privileged to write this chapter for *Catch Fire* to assist you with finding a greater level of health as you attain your wealth! First, though, I would like to share with you a little about myself. I graduated from college in Edmonton, Alberta, Canada, in the Health and Wellness Industry with a focus in the alternative health care. After college I developed a very successful private practice where I worked with everyone from high-level professional athletes to people suffering from a health challenge or disease who wanted to regain their wellbeing. I focused on both nutrition and physical wellbeing through advanced massage therapy. To become a Registered Massage Therapist (RMT) in Canada (in most areas) requires a two-year-plus program. I took the option to enroll as a fulltime student and did two years in one. I graduated top of my class. To be an RMT also requires a license from the Province to practice as a Therapist. A few years after establishing a successful practice, I returned to class and studied nutrition to add to the value I could provide my clients.

Before I moved to the U.S., I retired from my practice. But even if I had not, none of my schooling or certificates would mean anything here simply because they are not transferable. Even if they were, many of you would not be impressed. As a nutritional coach, I have no fancy initials behind my name. The reason for that is simple: When I looked into going to school to be a 'Nutritionist' I looked into University only to find that even if you took extra-curricular courses outside of the training, they could limit what I could teach my clients and what solutions I could suggest for them. Like most universities, they are funded by INDUSTRIES. I was not interested in being taught a curriculum based on the Pharmaceutical, Dairy, Beef, and Wheat Industry's interests. I wanted to be able to bring people the truth. It's comparable to the kid's cereal commercial. Have you seen it? The one that touts that Corn Pops, Captain Crunch, and Trix are a great serving of WHOLE GRAINS! I nearly laid an egg when I first saw that commercial!! I was not going to be a part of the monopoly of large industry lying to the public. So instead of attending a formal university, I took several classes, courses, and worked closely with a mentor of mine who has a PhD and a Masters in Ayurvedic and Macrobiotic Nutrition. With that said, those of you interested in true health read on; those of you more concerned with initials behind my name, feel free to skip this chapter.

Focusing on Health

I believe that when a nation focuses on health, a healthier nation results. I feel that a quiet revolution is finally beginning here in the States. More and more people are taking back control and responsibility of their health, getting self-educated, and making better choices. Take Colorado, which is statistically considered the "healthiest state" in the U.S. Why? Because it emphasizes and focuses on a healthier lifestyle. It all starts with the individual. If YOU focus on your health, you can be a part of changing the nation rather than being a statistic! Statistics like these:

According to OECD Health Data: {4}

Organization of Economic Co-operation and Development

In 2005, obesity in the U.S. was the highest in the world at 30.6%.

Canada had an obesity rate of 14.3%

France had an obesity rate of 9.4%

According to a 2008 study by the Center for Disease Control (CDC),

Colorado has an obesity rate of 18.5%. {3}

NOTE: Obesity is defined as a body mass index (BMI) of 30 or greater. BMI is calculated from a person's weight and height and provides a reasonable indicator of body fatness and weight categories that may lead to health problems. Obesity is a major risk factor for cardiovascular disease, certain types of cancer, and type 2 diabetes. {CDC}

According the CDC in 2005-2006: {3}

67% of Americans were categorized as Overweight or Obese.

It also stated that the top five killers in the U.S. in that same year were:

1. Heart Disease

2. Cancer

3. Stroke

4. Respiratory

5. Diabetes

From 1975 to 2003, we saw an increase of the occurrence of nearly all cancers. In 2003, we saw a plateau for some and in 2006 we saw a 2% decline. Many now say "we are winning the war against cancer." WOW. I am not a pessimist but I am a realist. We are not winning, not even close. It would be like losing a football game by 50 points and scoring one touchdown and saying we are winning the game. The decrease in cancer rates over the past few years is attributed to technological advances and early detection. If we really want to win....my question is this...what are we treating, the CAUSE or the SYMPTOM?

YOUR Current Health is
THE SUM OF YOUR CHOICES.
THERE ARE NO ACCIDENTS.

I believe all disease in the body occurs as a **SYMPTOM—a symptom** of poor lifestyle choices. These choices include things like poor nutrition and lack of exercise. Disease doesn't just one day knock on your door and say "hello, here I am!" In most cases, disease is a symptom of years and years and years and years of poor choices.

Now many of you cite your great-grandparents, grandparents, or even parents who ate bacon and eggs every day, smoked like a chimney, and lived to be 90 years old...or older. BUT remember that back then, most folks lived off their own land; food was not mass produced, not genetically altered, and not sprayed with dozens of different chemicals. Food was grown in soil that still contained all the nutrients needed for healthy eating.

After World War II, however, we saw a rapid decline in the nutrition available in the soil, which soon led, of course, to less nutritious foods. The primary reason for this happened after the war ended. Researchers discovered that the elements needed to create weapons—which were no longer needed in those mass quantities—could be used to manufacture cheap and easy fertilizer. What a DISCOVERY!! And it substantially changed the way in which we grew our food.

Rather than "working the land", it was much easier and cheaper to just throw down some fertilizer. Now our soil has become rich in nitrogen, potassium, and phosphorus, all three necessary for a plant to grow. But for us humans, that's another story. Because we are complex beings, we require far more than just these three nutrients to keep us healthy and vital. We require other vitamins, trace minerals, and the antioxidants that occur from the natural growing process. In terms of being far less healthy, we now live with the negative effects of our nutrient-depleted foods (not to mention our obsession with junk food and fast food).

Over time, these poor choices take a toll on the make-up and the strength of our genetics. GENETICS!! *(I am mildly psychic and know that some of you were already playing that card in your head.)* We ALL have our own family histories; we all have been passed down a genetic code. Almost everyone can simply refer to their family to see family members with cancer, diabetes, etc. This is not the sole factor in your fate. Picture your health as a chain. Your chain my have a few 'weak links'…but do those weak links have to break? I submit to you that they do NOT. By merely maintaining healthy choices you can avoid 'breaking those weak links.' But if you abuse the chain by making poor choices…they will most likely break, and the cycle continues as you pass on the habits of abuse and poor choices. To prove that our choices are harming our children, and even more so our children's children, all I have to appeal to is your memory, then I will get to the statistics.

Remember when there was only one "fat kid" in the class? Remember when asthma was a weird and rare disease, one that maybe one kid in the whole school suffered from? Remember when you didn't know anyone with diabetes? Obviously if you are in your 20's or younger, this will not be true for you. For everyone else, it will certainly be true.

Let's get to statistics:

> CDC reports: Data collected and analyzed by The National Health and Nutrition Examination Survey (NHANES)
>
> Data from NHANES surveys (1976–1980 and 2003–2006) show that the prevalence of obesity has increased:
>
> - for children aged 2–5 years, prevalence increased from 5.0% to 12.4%;
>
> - for those aged 6–11 years, prevalence increased from 6.5% to 17.0%;
>
> - and for those aged 12–19 years, prevalence increased from 5.0% to 17.6% {4}
>
> Statistically In the United States, between 1980 and 2004 obesity prevalence doubled among adults.
>
> Remember… "Obesity is associated with increased risk of a number of conditions, including diabetes mellitus, cardiovascular disease, hypertension, and certain cancers, and with increased risk of disability and a modestly elevated risk of all-cause mortality." {CDC}

Our lifestyle choices have drastically shifted our health and the health of our children. Pop-tarts and Captain Crunch for breakfast, peanut butter and white bread sandwiches for lunch, and fast food or pizza for dinner is killing us and our children. Disease is not a surprise visitor; it is the consequence of daily laziness, poor habits, and an emphasis on convenience.

YOU HAVE A CHOICE TO MAKE!

Here's the good news: you can make the CHOICE to become healthier. You can stick with ease and comfort NOW…and spend your early retirement years battling diseases, the side effects from drugs, and other un-pleasantries. Or, you can make a serious and committed effort NOW so you actually experience **longevity with health and vitality.**

This book, *Catch Fire*, attempts to give you a great big WAKE UP call in the area of your financial future. Even more, it has the information you need to move forward in a different and better direction. This is PRICELESS. In reality, however, most people are too sick, tired, or rundown to even have the ENERGY it will require to create financial freedom, and even if they do, no matter how much wealth they create, they cannot enjoy it if they are sick, dying, or dead!

This moment is about a great big wake up call when it comes to your health! Please answer the following questions honestly:

Do you CURRENTLY feel tired or fatigued in the middle of the day?

Do you frequently get colds or flu's?

Do you have joint or muscle pain?

Do you suffer from frequent headaches or migraines?

If you said yes to two or more of these, you are in the very beginning stages of creating 'dis-ease' in your body. Even if you feel you are "healthy" by North American standards, you could probably still greatly improve your health. Remember, it doesn't matter how young or old you are, you health is YOUR responsibility!

Good health can be yours *regardless of your current health situation.* No matter how old or sick you are right now, it is possible to regain your health. The body is DESIGNED to heal itself. The **process of regeneration** occurs literally every moment in your body. EVERY cell that is currently in your body RIGHT now at this moment WILL be replaced by a NEW cell within days, weeks, months, or this year. Each cell in your body is formed from the lifestyle choices you have made. Please realize that *years of the SAME type of choices will determine the strength or weaknesses in your health.*

If TODAY you are NOT as strong or healthy as you once were, you are not regenerating, you are **degenerating**. Telltale signs of the beginning of degeneration are fatigue, muscle and joint pain, regular colds and flu's, and headaches. Disease is chronic degeneration; it is, in other words, poor choices over a long period of time.

Again, the good news is that anyone can turn their health around and feel energetic, vital, and happy. You see, each time a new cell is formed, it will be made up of the tools you give your body just like the strength and durability of a house depends on the quality of the materials used to build it.

To ensure that you start to regenerate again and replace your current cells with ones that are stronger and superior, you MUST give your body the RIGHT tools.

3 KEYS to Longevity with Health and Vitality

"Health is a state of complete physical, mental and social well-being, and not merely the absence of disease or infirmity."

I believe three components must be in place for you to experience the highest levels of health. All three of these elements are important, yet one stands out due to its radical influence over the other two.

In order of importance, these health components are:

1. Nutrition

2. Exercise

3. Spiritual, Mental Health or Attitude

Now I am SURE MANY of you just got very upset. How can I put nutrition before spirituality??!! Before you slam shut this book, let me tell you my story.

In my early twenties, I suffered from an eating disorder. I would binge at night and then TRY to purge. (I never figured out how to make myself puke. I wish I could have done it. It certainly wasn't for lack of trying!) All day I would eat PERFECTLY. At night, however, my wolf came out. (At least that's what it felt like.) I would literally go HUNTING for food to eat. Since I didn't stock cookies, cakes, etc. in my apartment, I would literally go out and find some at the corner store, coffee house, or grocery store. I would rush back home with my kill and eat till I almost burst. It was a nightmare. It was a dark time and it wasn't easy. Willpower wasn't enough to tame the wolf inside me. This "hunger" felt insatiable, like an empty pit in my stomach that couldn't be filled. This lasted a good year before I admitted I had a problem and needed help. And as it so often happens, when you seek you shall find! Help arrived! It arrived in the form of high density, super absorbable nutrition program. Within ONE WEEK of beginning this program, my cravings disappeared. My inner wolf had been BANISHED. It felt like nothing short of a miracle!

After two months, I had lost 20 lbs and I had NEVER felt better. I felt SO good I decided I was going to train for a triathlon.

Let me give you some background. On the playground at recess I was the kid who got picked LAST. I was the kid that forged fake doctors' notes to get out of gym class. I had not ridden a bike since junior high. I did NOT finish swimming lessons and I HATED running! Despite all this, I trained for nine months, I completed a triathlon, an achievement I am still very proud of to this day. But I could not have maintained the mental and physical endurance of nine moths of training and accomplished my target had I not been feeding my body correctly!

My mind was so clear, my energy boundless, and my spirit never felt lighter, more connected, and free! It felt like an awakening! Food truly was the doorway to the heart! Who knew! But it has to be the RIGHT type of food.

You see, my body was lacking in some very important nutrients. When I gave my body the right tools, WOW—it had an astounding effect on my mental and spiritual health! This experience sparked my passion for nutrition and its effects on our health. It was after this pivotal point in my life I got more educated. I took classes and courses on nutrition and the effects food has on the INSIDE of the body. I studied like my life depended on it, because it very well does.

I believe our bodies are but a vessel for our time here on earth, and if we were meant for good and great things, we were also meant to take care of that vessel so we CAN accomplish our own individual purposes.

> *"Or do you not know that your body is a temple of the*
> *Holy Spirit within you, whom you have from God?*
> *You are not your own, for you were bought with a price.*
> *So glorify God in your body."*
> 1 Corinthians 6:19 (ESV)

1. NUTRITION – THE RIGHT TOOLS

Let's get into some brass tacks. I keep my nutrition keys very BASIC. Our body doesn't like complicated, it never has. So what I am about to share with you isn't sexy, it's simple. It isn't fancy, it's fundamental!

> *"Success is like a coin with two sides to it, one is fundamentals, and the other is distinctions. Master the "Fundamentals"*
> *and seek out the distinctions-*
> *one will not take you to the finish line- you need both!"*
> –Rock Thomas
>
> In achieving vitality and health there are several fundamentals, the distinctions you will figure out as you go. Each person is unique and therefore there is NO "one size fits all" when it comes to the distinctions of your health! Start with the Fundamentals, then seek out your distinctions!

The THREE TOOLS

The three tools your body needs are OXYGEN, WATER, and NUTRIENTS.

OXYGEN obviously comes from breathing and from EXERCISE (we'll get to exercise in a moment). To show you how important oxygenation is to your body, here are two excerpts from the papers of Dr. Otto Warburg, one of the twentieth century's leading biochemists:

> "All normal cells have an absolute requirement for oxygen, but cancer cells CAN live WITHOUT oxygen - a rule without exception."

"Deprive a cell 60% of its oxygen and it will turn cancerous. Deprive a cell 35% of its oxygen for 48 hours and it may become cancerous."

***Otto Heinrich Warburg (October 8, 1883 - August 1, 1970) {1}

WATER is essential to our health. If the ONLY thing you did for your health was to give up coffee, soda pop, juices, etc. and JUST drank enough water everyday, you would see a DRASTIC change in your health in short order!

Your body is 60 – 70% water, meaning that if you aren't drinking enough water; your body will begin to breakdown. Dehydrated cells don't function properly.

Dehydration also causes headaches and hunger pains. When people should just be drinking water, they are often eating instead. And most are eating foods high in sodium that TAKE water from the body…hence why you still feel hungry after that bag of chips, loaf of bread, or bowl of pasta. I am sure you can guess what all the eating leads to.

How much should you drink? Take your body weight in pounds, and then divide it in half; that is how many ounces a day you should drink. If you exercise regularly; drink coffee, alcohol, or soda pop; or travel in planes a lot, you should drink more.

Carry a bottle of water wherever you go (preferably one you can re-use or RECYCLE!).

NUTRIENTS come from the food we eat. As humans, we ONLY need the following five nutrients to stay healthy and vital (these nutrients are the building blocks of our cells and therefore our health):

- Vitamins

- Minerals

- Carbohydrates

- Amino Acids (make up protein)

- And a little bit of the RIGHT types of FATS.

- Fiber (Fiber is not actually one of the five nutrients, but it is essential for many functions in your body and for your overall health.)

***ALL of these can be found in FRESH and ORGANIC fruits, vegetables, beans, legumes, nuts and seeds.

You have all heard "We are what we eat…." Most Americans would be repulsed if they actually knew the true contents in our processed "food." Aside from all the additives, preservatives, fillers, colors, and toxins added to our processed food, let me give you just <u>one</u> frightening example. California's Central Valley is a Mecca for TWO things, growing fruits and vegetables and making crystal meth (that's right, the drug). Unfortunately, in order to make one pound of methamphetamine, six pounds of corrosive liquids, acid vapors, heavy metals, solvents and other harmful materials are also created. Whether made in a garage, basement, or the back of a van, these homemade scientists are not environmentally friendly; they dump the dangerous waste just about anywhere they want in the Central Valley. An agent with the Federal Bureau of Investigation (FBI) is known to have said, "Millions of pounds of toxic chemicals are going into the fruit basket of the United States. The chemicals are turning up in alarming levels in ground-water samples."

We are what we eat, but we are more truthfully **WHAT WE ABSORB!** Most North Americans have an average of 9 – 12 pounds of old fermenting fecal matter in their colon at all times. This literally "cakes" the walls of our intestines, rendering the vitally important 'villi' from absorbing the nutrients from our foods. Instead they absorb the toxic waste. So instead of nutrients being shuttled into our blood stream to necessary locations throughout the body, we instead receive toxins from our old fecal matter! Are you getting a visual yet?

This fecal compacting occurs primarily because of the fast food, junk food, and processed food revolution. Chips, crackers, pasta, cookies, breads, pastries, microwave food, instant meals, and canned foods all are missing the RIGHT TOOLS. They have practically no nutritional value in regards to vitamins and minerals; they are HIGH in sodium, so they take water from the body. And also just as important they have practically NO real fiber to speak of, not the type your colon needs to scrub itself clean! These processed foods act like GLUE in your intestines. Most processed foods have SOME sort of FLOUR as a main ingredient. Again, I am going to appeal to your memory. Remember way back when you mixed flour and water. What did you get? GLUE! Glue to put up wall paper, glue to create Paper Mache art with your kids! THAT is exactly what is clogging up your colon, fermenting and leeching TOXINS and waste RIGHT into your BLOOD stream. It's the reason why people feel tired during the day, get headaches, and just plain feel CRAPPY. It is also the reason people get "the FARTS" after eating fresh veggies. It is a sign your digestive system is so compromised you cannot digest the MOST NATURAL foods in the world. Years and years of these poor food choices will eventually lead to disease.

Long-term HEALTH begins with a clean and functioning colon, and to have one of those you MUST start eating NUTRIENT RICH and FIBER-filled foods! I will cover more on this in the next section.

This is Crucial: pH & nutrition

Basically your body is a BIG chemistry set. It is a complex series of trillions of chemical reactions going on every moment of everyday. These chemical reactions never stop. (Don't worry, I promised I will keep things simple!) Your body is always trying to achieve ONE THING, and that is BALANCE. Its balance is measured in all different ways: blood oxygen levels, potassium to sodium levels, which kind and how much bacteria is present in our colon, the acidity of our stomach, the list could go on and on. The balance element I find that trumps them all is your pH level. Why? You see, the pH of the body is a CRUCIAL element to ALL the chemical reactions that occur in your body. If your pH is "off" those reactions that keep you alive and well will slow or stop, causing 'things' to begin to breakdown. A healthy body likes to be a **7.3**…JUST slightly alkaline! (It is important to know that your saliva, stomach, skin, and urine SHOULD be on the acidic side, which is natural and normal!)

ACID   The pH Scale   ALKALINE

0 1 2 3 4 5 6 7 8 9 10 11 12 13 14

Soda: 2.5, Coffee: 3.8, Beer: 4.5, Pure Water: 7,
Human Blood: 7.5, Broccoli/Spinach 8, Green Drink: 10

Exponential Factor. It is important to know that on the pH scale, 7 is NEUTRAL, and each number higher or lower is exponentially MORE acidic or alkaline than the one before.

8 is 10x MORE alkaline than 7

9 is 100x MORE alkaline than 7

10 is 1000x more alkaline than 7

11 is 10,000x more alkaline than 7…

I think you get the idea; the same works the other way.

Now that you know this, take another look at the scale. At around 2.5, soda is approximately 10,000 times more acidic than the body wants to be to maintain health. WOW, talk about detrimental! And don't forget, soda has 11–16 teaspoons of sugar present, which basically shuts down your immune system for a full four hours and puts your pancreas in overdrive. They might as well label it "Diabetes in a Can"! Diet soda is NO better; instead of getting processed sugar, you get MANUFACTURED sugar! Remember how I said the body does NOT like complicated? Well, any manufactured food is too complicated for your body to deal with. Manufactured food is essentially a toxin or foreign substance not recognized by your body. This is bad news over a long period of time. Because it is SUCH a huge industry, you will see ALL kinds of studies and pharmaceutical companies and even doctors say that manufactured sugar is safe!!!

What determines the pH of your body? The foods you eat! Imagine for a moment that your body is a FIREPLACE and the food you eat is WOOD. When the wood is set on fire and burned, there is a residue: ASH. Same with your food! As your digestive system breaks down and burns the food, it leaves an ASH and THAT ash will find itself somewhere on the pH scale. It will be either Acidic or Alkaline in nature, which will then have an effect on the pH of your blood!

Disease CANNOT flourish in an ALKALINE body. It is impossible.

Remember, we are a chemistry set!

It takes approximately 10 fresh salads to offset the acidity from a steak.

So over and above ANY other fad, diet, or advice, I say eating ALKALINE is by far one of the MOST IMPORTANT things you can do for your body, PERIOD!

RULE of THUMB: Stay as CLOSE to the 'garden patch' as POSSIBLE! It is what your body knows! That means a LOT of FRESH (and ORGANIC):

- Fruits and Vegetables

- Nuts and Seeds (not the salted snack mixes either)

- Cooked or sprouted whole grains like oats, kamut, quinoa, brown rice, and millet.

- Cooked or sprouted legumes like red, green and black lentils.

- Cooked or sprouted beans.

Below is a LIST of BOTH Alkaline forming foods and Acidic-forming foods.

FOODS that leave a neutral or ALKALINE ash in the BODY are:

VEGETABLES:

Aduki Beans	Asparagus	Beans, lentils
Beets	Broccoli	Brussel Sprouts
Cabbage	Carrots	Cauliflower
Celery	Garlic	Green Beans
Lettuce	Lima Beans	Molasses
Mushrooms	Onions	Parsley
Parsnips	Peas	Potatoes
Radishes	Rutabagas	Sauerkraut
Sea Vegtables (sea weed)	Spinach	Soybeans
Sprouts	Squash	Tomatoes (Raw)
Turnips		

FRUITS:

Apples	Apricots	Avocados
Bananas	Blackberries	Cantaloupe
Cherries	Coconut	Dates
Figs	Grapefruit	Grapes
Lemons	Oranges	Peaches
Pears	Pineapple	Raisins
Raspberries	Strawberry	Watermelon

GRAINS:

Quinoa	Amaranth	Buckwheat
Millet	Sprouted Grains	

NUTS:

Almonds	Brazil Nuts	Flax Seeds
Pumpkin Seeds	Sunflower Seeds	

FOODS that leave an ACIDIC ash in the body are:

POOR ACID FOODS:

Flour- All	Cranberries	Refined Sugars
Dairy- All, cheese, milk, sour cream, yogurt, etc.	Fish- All	Meat –All, pork, beef etc…
Plums	Poultry - All, chicken, turkey, duck, etc.	Prunes

OTHER HIGHLY ACID FORMING 'FOODS' OR FACTORS:

Alcohol	Coffee	Soda Pop
Sugar	Synthetic Vitamins	Chemical Additives
Drugs, Prescribed & Recreational	Stress	

BETTER ACID FOODS (only slightly acidic)

Barley	Blueberries	Corn
Honey	Nuts	Oatmeal
Whole Grain Pasta	Rice	Soy Products (in moderation)

As you can see, the foods that make up 90 percent of a typical North American diet (meat, dairy, flour products, coffee, alcohol, and soda pop) are HIGHLY acidic. This is a recipe for disease and the continuation of the degeneration of the integrity of your health.

Even worse, the AMOUNTS of dairy, meat, and processed foods consumed is unreal and unnecessary! So YES, I am telling you this plain and simple: EAT LESS MEAT and DAIRY. I mean DRASTICALLY reduce how much you eat of these and exponentially INCREASE your fresh fruit and vegetables! I know that some of you just CHECKED OUT! Give up meat, dairy, etc? No way! Understand, there is no right or wrong to your decision to follow this advice, only consequences—consequences like arthritis, high blood pressure, cholesterol, heart disease, and compromised digestion, all of which leads to 'dis-ease' in the body. Your choice.

ALKALINE foods also happen to be:

1. NUTRIENT-rich

2. Full of the good kinds of FIBER

3. Full of the good kinds of FATS

4. And are low-glycemic

The IMPORTANCE of the RIGHT FOODS and RIGHT FATS!

The right kinds of Fiber and Fat can help to keep your cholesterol levels low, support proper digestion and help you maintain a healthy weight. The *right* types of fats keep your brain activity healthy and help your body absorb other essential nutrients. They have also been proven to help your body burn fat and prevent cancer!! This is very unlike the bad fats, which cause obesity, high cholesterol and high blood pressure, just to mention a few! I feel this is SO important for you to know that I created a chart to simplify the subjects of GOOD fats and BAD FATS for you!

These are listed in order of MOST healthy for your to LEAST healthy for you.

GOOD FATS:	SOURCES
Monounsaturated	NUTS: walnuts, almonds, peanuts, pistachios. Seeds, avocado, leafy greens, bananas, wild salmon, olive oil.
Polyunsaturated	Sunflower seeds and oil, soy beans and oil, nuts, avocado, oatmeal, canola and olive oil.

These good fats will help you burn fat and lose weight. They will help to lower cholesterol (total and LDL). Prevent cancer, Lou Gehrig's (ALS) disease and heart disease. They will improve MANY of your body's function.

BAD FATS:	SOURCES
Saturated	All Animal products All meat, beef, pork, chicken, turkey etc… All dairy, eggs, fish, seafood Coconut and Kernel oil
Trans Fats / Hydrogenated oils	Most processed and packaged foods Margarine, lard, microwave popcorn, french fries, chips, crackers, cookies, baked goods.

Bad fats are detrimental to the body, especially when eaten daily. The body cannot process these.

Saturated fats build up in our arteries…not just at the heart, in the brain, in the legs, but also the liver or kidneys. They CAUSE heart disease and obesity.

Trans fats are just plain dangerous. Health organizations worldwide have warned consumers to consumer only TRACE amounts as they have been linked to cancers and diseases that attack the nervous system.

When grocery shopping, **CHECK the LABELS** for "hydrogenated," "hydrolyzed" and saturated fats and avoid those foods!

When it comes to eating right and exercising, there is no
"I'll start tomorrow." Tomorrow is disease.
~Terri Guillemets

To REGAIN Health (currently suffering from disease):
a ratio of 90% alkaline and 10% acidic food choices

If you're in good health and to take it to a new level:
a ratio of 80% alkaline to 20% acidic

To MAINTAIN current GREAT health:
a ratio of 70% alkaline foods and 30% acidic

Exercise

*"Those who do not make time for exercise will
have to make time for illness."*
~Earl of Derby

Exercise is NECESSARY and ESSENTIAL to your long term health and vitality. We USED to be hunters, gatherers, farmers and settlers. Most of our days were spent being physical. NOW most North Americas are completely sedentary. Most go from their beds to their desks to the couch, and then they rinse and repeat. This is the opposite of what our bodies need to stay UPRIGHT and healthy!

Exercise must be a regular part of your day, like brushing your teeth. It also must include BOTH cardiovascular activities and strengthening activities.

JUST to maintain your BONE density, skeletal health, and upright posture you MUST be doing something that challenges and strengthens the muscles, such as weight-bearing exercise. Because there is no land to till, homes to be built, bales to haul, rocks to remove, or food to be harvested, many now go to a place called a GYM where there are other people picking up and moving bars with weights on them! You have to laugh! But nonetheless, y**our MUSCLES are the KEY to the Energy production in your body and to your metabolism.** So strong, healthy and supple muscles will not only keep you energetic throughout the day, they will help to "burn" fat! Certain types of yoga are also great for strengthening.

To maintain a healthy HEART and oxygenation in the blood, you must be doing some regular yet challenging cardiovascular activities. Examples include a brisk walk, running, biking, rollerblading, and swimming, dancing or skipping. Getting involved with a team or learning a sport like tennis, basketball, football, racquetball or hockey also promotes physical activity. There are so many fun ways to give your heart a great workout!

Changing up your fitness program every three to four months is important to challenging the body and keep it adapting. When you do this, your body has to create new neuro-pathways! It's a great way to keep your brain and your body young! Learning and doing something NEW regularly will accomplish this. Take surfing lessons, or dust off the bike you haven't touched in years! If you always do the same activity or routine, you will actually begin to breakdown the body and create "occupational injuries."

Your fitness program should fit your targets. A fitness program to lose weight would be completely different than the one to build muscle mass. A fitness program for a beginner would be completely different than one of a seasoned pro. It would be different if you had a back, neck, or knee injury to consider. In other words, I can't give you a one-size-fits-all fitness program. It is important to fit your program to your unique targets and needs.

My HIGHEST suggestion (or, if it helps, consider this an ORDER) is to find a REPUTABLE establishment where you can meet up with a registered and licensed Personal Fitness Trainer. INVEST in yourself, your health, and your SAFETY! Pay a few extra bucks to get a consultation, review your targets, and have them CREATE a personalized fitness program that includes both cardio and strength training! Be sure to do a couple private training sessions where they TAKE you through the MOTIONS of your program so you know what you are doing! If you have "issues" around that, get OVER it! It is FAR more important to your health you execute each exercise correctly than injure yourself because you were too shy or too proud. Three to four months later, go BACK for a re-evaluation, and then have them create a new program based on your progress. Be sure to do another couple sessions to get comfortable with the new program. Presto—you're good for another three to four months!

Honestly, it is one on the BEST investments you can make in your physical health. This is approximately a $350 investment every three to four months. It's WORTH it! YOU are worth it! Obesity, disease and ALL the health risks that come from being sedentary will cost you FAR more than that; especially here in the U.S.

Spirituality

You may be surprised what an effect feeding your body the right tools and exercising will have on your spiritual life, mental health, and overall attitude! Whenever I fall off the "health bandwagon", I get irritable, tired, and negative.

While spirituality, mental health, and attitude can be focused on individually, remember that we are WHOLISTIC BEINGS. Our body, mind, and our soul are INTERCONNECTED, meaning each part affects the other. If you treat yourself as a multi-faceted being, you will feel better than you ever have in your entire life.

Many North Americans get so caught up in the rat race or in the process of creating wealth, they forget to nurture this part of themselves. In order to be a happy, healthy human being, you cannot ignore feeding your soul; you must connect at a deep level with others and your God. If you do not, you will eventually (in some shape or form) sabotage yourself and your success. **So take care of your soul!**

Another issue that many people deal with is "storing" incidents from the past or negative emotions in their body. Now to some of you that might sound weird, to others you may already know the science behind it. Each cell has a form of cellular memory. It passes this memory on from cell to cell to cell. Thus specific incidents or a series of repeated incidents can be programmed into our cells, similar to downloading software onto your computer. It will run until you uninstall it. These negative emotions or incidents can be as simple as hearing "fat jokes" at home and school while growing up, to as serious as sexual abuse or being the victim of rape.

Holding on to an emotional memory can be detrimental to your body, mind, and spirit, and causes MANY people to carry extra weight as protection or barrier. If you feel you might be doing this yourself, I implore you to find help. Traditional therapy, hypnotherapy, emotional release therapies like Cranial Sacral Therapy can be found in almost any area. Healing is a part of re-connecting and connection is the essence of spirituality.

In Closing

Your health is your responsibility. You can take control now or be a victim later, it's up to you. If your priorities include living a long full life, being there for your children 100%, achieving a high level of success, or just plain feeling fantastic all the time, this will require you to make a commitment to your health. It will require you to MAKE time to take care of yourself. It will require you to break old bad habits and create new ones that support your vision and purpose. It won't be easy for some of you, but I know you can do it because I did it. I was junk food junkie when I was a kid, and I hated exercise. Now I am a health nut and love to move my body! I went from shy and awkward to powerful and confident by following the elements within this chapter!

No matter where you are at now with your health, you can RE-commit, RE-start, and RE-invent yourself and your future healthy self! I believe in you!

If you would like a health consultation, healthy recipes, review your targets, and make a plan, you can contact me at customhealth4you@catchfireuniversity.com

SUGGESTED READING:

Eat To Live: The Revolutionary Plan for Fast and Sustained Weight Loss By Joel D Fuhrman M.D., www.drfuhrman.com

Anything by Neal D. Barnard, M.D.
Author of books such as *EAT RIGHT LIVE LONGER, Breaking the food Seduction, Turn off the Fat genes, The Cancer survivors guide,* etc.... www.nealbarnard.org/books.cfm

The pH Miracle for weight loss, Dr. Robert Young, www.phmiracleliving.com

Alkalize or Die, Dr T.A Baroody Jr.

RESOURCES:

1. The Prime Cause and Prevention of Cancer
   Dr. Otto Warburg
   Lecture delivered to Nobel Laureates on June 30, 1966

2. The Prime Cause and Prevention of Cancer
   with two prefaces on prevention

3. Centre of Disease Control website
   http://www.cdc.gov/obesity/data/index.html (accessed March 29, 2010)

http://www.cdc.gov/nchs/fastats/overwt.htm (accessed March 28, 2010)

4. NationMaster.com
    http://www.nationmaster.com/graph/hea_obe-health-obesity#source (accessed March 28, 2010)

5. Health Canada website

6. National Institute of Cancer http://seer.cancer.gov/report_to_nation/   (accessed April 30, 2010)

7. Wikipedia (accessed May 2, 2010)

Epilogue

Now what? Well, you are at a moment of choice. You can go back to the way you were, or you can do some things differently. Some who read this book have already made a choice: they have justified not changing. Maybe they found a job or have heard on the news the economy is getting better, and they can now slip back in to the way things were, i.e., "comfortably miserable." With the risk of sounding like "Johnny rain cloud," I can promise you the economy will get better and then it will get worse and then guess what? It will get better again. It has always done this and will continue to do so. One thing I can promise you is this: if the future is to be better than the present, you must make your decision based on what's best for the future. It's simple but it's not always easy. True fulfillment and reward is never reserved for those that make the easy choices. Obstacles are to be expected and even *embraced* if you want to succeed at this journey. There is so much to learn about this game of money and life. This book was designed to be a wake up call and to give you the basic but transformational tools to begin your journey to freedom. This book was a start. I could have written an encyclopedia but I'm pretty sure it wouldn't have been published. If you do not embrace the basics, freedom will never be yours.

I know some of you are ready! Ready to tackle the information and learn to the rules of the game and begin to play to thrive, not just survive. For those people we have created the **Catch Fire University**, where you can learn from some of the greatest minds in the world. The University will do what a book can never accomplish: to be interactive, experiential and fun. It is highly educational and will gently force you to accomplish your targets.

You can come to one of two conclusions. You can decide that you are capable of learning the skills to lead a happy prosperous life, or that you are simply a victim to the economy or whatever circumstances arrive. I pray you choose the first.

I realize that I can be a bit blunt. Don't confuse my directness for a lack of compassion. I believe in the power of people, the power of love and the power that lies within you and all of us. I believe in my heart of hearts that if you are reading these words, you already posses all the raw material to create a masterpiece of a life. I cannot believe for a second that anyone was put on this earth to live between alarm clocks and time clocks. We all have a purpose; we are each here for a good reason. Those reasons lie in your dreams. At the beginning of this book I dedicated it to all those who are committed to their dreams, so for those of you that are, let's share the good within us in a BIG way! Understand that the quickest and most effective way of doing that is to get the money thing out of the way. Creating freedom is a process of removing the limitations, restrictions and shackles of the financial prison. Once you do that, you will be unbridled and your dreams liberated.

I have shared with you the playbook of getting STARTED. There is, however, a lot more to do. I hope you will join me and my team of experts to walk you through this exciting, sometimes scary, but always fulfilling journey. I hope to see you soon!!!!

About This Book

For many years people have been suggesting Doug write a book about his experience and life, and not unlike everything Doug does, once he decided to write this book, he committed to it entirely. There is so much of the recovery story that is yet untold, so many pivotal moments, learns and insights yet to share on how true lasting success can be created, so many experts to introduce to you. This book is the beginning.

To order additional copies of this book or to learn more about Doug and all that Catch Fire has to offer, visit us at www.CatchFireBook.com.

For more information

Visit our website at www.CatchFireUniversity.com

The link to join our **Community Mailing List** to receive announcements, special offers and free stuff is on our homepage!

Join our **Online Facebook Community** by Searching for Catch Fire

Follow our Blog at www.catchfirebook.blogspot.com

About Doug Nelson

Doug Nelson's story is a quintessential rags-to-riches journey. His experience as a child growing up in poverty became the catalyst that made him decide he would create his own wealth and freedom. When he was 23, Doug started the first of many successful businesses. By age 34, he was completely financially free.

At 35, Doug lived through an event that would forever change his life—he was in a serious natural gas explosion. Coming back from the brink of death and spending a year in rehabilitation, Doug realized the power of his unique financial situation. His passion and his mission became teaching people "How to Ignite their Own Economy" so that no matter what happens in their life, they are financially bulletproof. He has taught tens of thousands of students all over North America the principals and skills of creating Financial Freedom. Doug and his wife are currently creating an online curriculum called the Catch Fire University: Making Money a Learning Experience.

Doug currently resides in northern Minnesota with his wife, Melanie, and two dogs, Cash and Prosper.

BUY A SHARE OF THE FUTURE IN YOUR COMMUNITY

These certificates make great holiday, graduation and birthday gifts that can be personalized with the recipient's name. The cost of one S.H.A.R.E. or one square foot is $54.17. The personalized certificate is suitable for framing and will state the number of shares purchased and the amount of each share, as well as the recipient's name. The home that you participate in "building" will last for many years and will continue to grow in value.

Here is a sample SHARE certificate:

HABITAT FOR HUMANITY

THIS CERTIFIES THAT

YOUR NAME HERE

HAS INVESTED IN A HOME FOR A DESERVING FAMILY

1985-2010

TWENTY-FIVE YEARS OF BUILDING FUTURES
IN OUR COMMUNITY ONE HOME AT A TIME

1200 SQUARE FOOT HOUSE @ $65,000 = $54.17 PER SQUARE FOOT
This certificate represents a tax deductible donation. It has no cash value.

YES, I WOULD LIKE TO HELP!

I support the work that Habitat for Humanity does and I want to be part of the excitement! As a donor, I will receive periodic updates on your construction activities but, more importantly, I know my gift will help a family in our community realize the dream of homeownership. **I would like to SHARE in your efforts against substandard housing in my community!** *(Please print below)*

PLEASE SEND ME _____ SHARES at $54.17 EACH = $ $_____

In Honor Of: _____

Occasion: (Circle One)   HOLIDAY   BIRTHDAY   ANNIVERSARY

       OTHER: _____

Address of Recipient: _____

Gift From: _____ *Donor Address:* _____

Donor Email: _____

I AM ENCLOSING A CHECK FOR $ $_____ PAYABLE TO HABITAT FOR HUMANITY <u>OR</u> PLEASE CHARGE MY VISA OR MASTERCARD *(CIRCLE ONE)*

Card Number _____ Expiration Date: _____

Name as it appears on Credit Card _____ Charge Amount $ _____

Signature _____

Billing Address _____

Telephone # Day _____ Eve _____

PLEASE NOTE: Your contribution is tax-deductible to the fullest extent allowed by law.
Habitat for Humanity • P.O. Box 1443 • Newport News, VA 23601 • 757-596-5553
www.HelpHabitatforHumanity.org